BE A REAL TEEN-AGER!

Be a
REAL
Teen-ager!

Warren W. Wiersbe

. . .

FLEMING H. REVELL COMPANY
WESTWOOD, NEW JERSEY

The material in chapters 4 and 8 appeared in a different form in *Moody Monthly*; and the material in chapter 6 also appeared in a different form in *Youth for Christ* magazine. I appreciate the willingness of the editors of these two publications to allow me to use this material in this book.

To my four prospective teen-agers—
DAVID,
CAROLYN,
BOBBY, and
JUDY

• • •

Preface

THIS BOOK IS for teen-agers (and adults who want to help teen-agers), but it contains some dangerous ideas.

The first is that today's teens are caught in a deadly conspiracy that could rob them of their adult happiness as well as their enjoyment of their teen years.

The second is that today's teens don't need sugar-coated advice from matinee idols; they need down-to-earth principles from real teen-agers. This book contains principles, not fancy slogans or bits of adult advice.

The third is that the best place to find these principles is in the Bible. Be prepared for a lot of Bible reading as you meet six Bible teen-agers and learn the principles that guided them to success. Frankly, I find that the Bible is the most exciting, practical Book in the world! And the teens of the Bible are the most wonderful teens in the world!

These ideas may not be new. I've been sharing them with thousands of teens and adults in youth conferences and seminars for the past several years, so I know they work.

I hope you'll let them work in your life.

WARREN WIERSBE

Contents

BE A REAL TEEN-AGER!

1

Wanted:
Real Teen-agers!

IT MAY BE bad psychology, but I'm going to begin this book with a warning. It's this: *there is a plot afoot to change you into an artificial adult instead of a real teen-ager.* There are subtle forces at work in your world that could rob you of the greatest thrill of your seven teen years—the thrill of just being yourself, of following the pattern God set for you, and of emerging someday into the adult world, ready for life.

After all, if you aren't a real teen-ager today, how can you ever be a real adult tomorrow? If you're living on substitutes now, how will you ever recognize and enjoy the real values of life when they come your way?

In many respects today's teen-agers are victims of mistakes that some adults have made, mistakes that society has picked up and promoted and about which you and I can do very little. But one thing you can do is recognize the forces that are at work, identify them, and learn to overcome them.

Before we talk about these forces, however, let's try to discover what a *real teen-ager* is.

I think the first characteristic of a real teen-ager is that *he has accepted himself*. He isn't trying to be a child (although there will be times when he'll act like a child); neither is he trying to be an adult. He has looked at himself in the mirror and said, "Friend, you are a teen-ager! This means seven years ahead of you when you'll be misunderstood, pushed, criticized, and perhaps even rejected. But you'll also be taught, loved, encouraged, and helped in many ways to become a balanced adult. Now, stick with the job of being yourself; grow up while you grow old, and discover the things that really count."

Too many teens these days celebrate their thirteenth birthday by jumping headlong into adult activities and privileges for which they simply aren't prepared. "I'm a teen-ager now, Mom. Can't I go steady?" Instead of accepting their teen years as a time of transition, a bridge between the dependence of childhood and the interdependence of adulthood, they immediately dive off the bridge into the river of life—and find themselves drowning in demands that are over their heads.

This is why so many young people develop emotional problems, create difficulties at home, and worse yet, get in trouble with the law. They're plugging their 6-volt toys into a 220-volt generator and blowing all their fuses before they really have a chance to live.

A real teen-ager, then, accepts the fact that he *is* a teen-ager, and that his main task in life is learning how to be an adult. He accepts himself, his strengths and weaknesses, his world around him, and the challenge God has placed in his hands. He's willing to wait for adult privileges. The rest of his crowd may run ahead, sneering as they pass him on the road of life; but the real teen-ager knows he'll catch up with them in a few years and find them bored with life, their dynamic all gone, while he's ready to move into the challenges of adulthood.

So, make up your mind right now that you're going to be a *real teen-ager*—not an artificial adult, not an actor, not a pretender. Make up your mind that you're going to *invest* in these teen years, and not just "spend them," knowing that your investments will pay big dividends in the years to come.

Now, don't get the idea that a real teen-ager sits on the sidelines and watches everybody else have the fun! Quite the contrary is true. The teen-ager who knows who he is, what he's supposed to do, and where he's going will always get more out of life than the "artificial adult" who is trying to be something God never meant him to be. After all, little Josephine can put mother's high heels on her little five-year-old feet, and wrap mother's best dress around her five-year-old body, but that won't make her an adult. She'll discover, instead, that the shoes keep her from making any progress and the dress has a way of making her fall. Transfer this scene to your high school campus and you'll understand why some of your "grown up" friends never seem to get anywhere and are usually falling into trouble.

No, the real teen-ager enjoys life a lot more than the teens who want to enjoy adult privileges before they're ready to accept adult responsibilities. The real teen-ager has that sense of stability that gives him poise and purpose, and that rescues him from embarrassing and even dangerous situations.

Something else is true of a real teen-ager: he not only accepts himself, but *he understands himself*. He realizes that important changes are going on in his body, his home, and his world. These changes don't frighten or perplex him because he understands where they came from and what the final results will be. Ignorance always leads to insecurity, but understanding leads to strength and stability.

Here is where the "artificial adult" suffers: he plunges into adult experiences without being able to handle them, and without really understanding all that's involved. These experiences become destructive instead of creative in his life, and he ends up in worse shape than when he started! Jesus said, "And ye shall know the truth, and the truth shall make you free" (John 8:32). But they ignore the truth, and the result is bondage.

A third characteristic of the real teen-ager is that *he lives with a serious purpose in mind*. He realizes that he must *employ* his teen years and not simply *enjoy* them; that he has a job to do during these seven important years, *a job that can be done at no other time in life.* If Johnny fails to learn some good habits while still at home, we hope the kindergarten teacher will straighten things out. Grade school problems can sometimes be solved in junior high school. But if you let your teen years slip through your fingers, you'll take into your adult life the weaknesses and problems that can be magnified and multiplied into adult failures. The old adage bears repeating: "What you are going to be, you are becoming right now."

A real teen-ager, then, accepts himself, understands himself, and directs himself by a serious purpose. There is one final characteristic: *a real teen-ager knows that he can't do the job alone.* You'll never hear him shout, "Leave me alone! I can run my own life!" He knows better. He knows that he needs his family, his friends, and his God if he's going to make a success of his teen years. He realizes that he'll have to follow the best possible examples, listen to the best possible counsel, and aim for the best possible goals.

That's why I've written this book. I want to share with you some basic principles that can make your teen years a thrilling success instead of a tragic failure—principles that deal with the down-to-earth affairs of your life. I want to introduce you to six teen-agers from the Bible—*real teen-agers*—and show you from their successes and failures how you can be a real teen-ager.

I have been living with these Bible teens for years now, and I want you to know them and learn the secrets that made them great. I want you to meet Joseph and let him tell you how you can make your dreams come true. I want David to explain how to prepare for a fantastic future. (After all, David started as a shepherd and ended up a king!) Daniel will share with you the secret of being a transformer instead of a conformer; and Mary will tell you how to have real dynamic in your life. I want Timothy to explain what it means to be diligent and get the job done; and finally, I want you to meet the Ideal Teenager, Jesus Christ, who will show you the perfect example of what a teen-ager ought to be.

But first, I promised to explain the forces at work in your world that are trying to rob you of your important teen years; so I'll do this in the next chapter. However, before you turn the page, tell yourself and God that, with His help, you're going to be, not an "artificial adult," but a real teen-ager.

2

Somebody's After You

PLEASE DON'T GET the idea that an adult mastermind in some hidden office is plotting the downfall of the American teen-ager. It really isn't that bad. But you had better recognize the fact that there are definite forces at work in your world, trying to rob you of your teen years. You and I may not be able to reform them, but at least we can learn to recognize and resist them.

All this fuss over the American teen-ager dates back to 1945, a post-war era when for the first time teen-agers moved into the spotlight. Of course, the war itself helped to bring this about. Thousands of teen-age boys were in uniform, and thousands more were helping the war effort at home. With millions of men away from home in the armed forces, the teens back home were on top of the population totem pole. They were Very Important People! Boys had to do men's work, so why shouldn't the boys be treated like men?

Another factor was the rise of juvenile delinquency. Nobody is quite sure what brought about the increase in teen-age crime, but one thing is sure: it put the teen-ager on the front page of every American newspaper and the public had to sit up and take notice. In fact, it almost came to the place where adults thought that "delinquent" and "teen-ager" were synonymous words! The end result was that people began to notice the younger generation and even began to be afraid of them!

The population explosion helped, too. From 1945 to the present, the world has seen an increase in population that has definitely affected every area of life. Big families became popular after World War II, and those new babies eventually became teen-agers.

Now, when a segment of the population begins to increase in size, get involved in serious problems, and raise new questions, the adults have to sit up and take notice. So, shortly after the war, people began to study the American teen-ager. Purdue University set up its "Public Opinion Poll" that resulted in the studies found in the book *The American Teen-ager*. Mr. Eugene Gilbert established his Gilbert Youth Survey organization and began telling the American public (through his newspaper column) what songs teens liked, what they ate, how they spent their leisure time, and what they felt should be done about the world situation. The field of adolescent psychology suddenly became important, and experts on teens began writing books for teachers, parents, and the teens themselves.

All of this led to a great opportunity for somebody to make a lot of money. After all, if you have millions of teen-agers, you also have millions of customers. And if these teens are starting to feel important in the world, why not assist them by treating them like adult customers? It was here that Big Business moved in, assisted by Big Advertising, and began that "artificial adult" propaganda that is ruining millions of young people today.

Here's how it works. Teens have money (Gilbert claims it averages out to about $10 per week for each teen) and this money has to be spent. The smart thing to do is to create a market. The result? Teen fashions, teen music, teen magazines, teen idols, and a vast array of items that today's teens think they cannot live without. The manufacturer knows that American young people spend over $10 billion a year, and he wants to get his fair slice of the watermelon. He knows that a steady teen customer is sure to become a steady adult customer, so his promotion to teens is a lifetime investment.

I believe that *Seventeen* was the first teen-age magazine to come out into mass circulation, and it was devoted primarily to helping girls become "mature teens." It was soon followed by a parade of "teen magazines" catering to the adolescent reader and most of these (and I believe there are about thirty on the newsstands now) revolve around teen matinee idols, fan clubs, date advice, self-help articles, and general news and views of the teen-age world. Some of them are close to becoming teen-age "confession" magazines, majoring in romance and sex, while other specialize in cars, careers, or culture. Your generation is the first in America to have so much "teen information" at your disposal.

The next step isn't difficult to understand: "teen-age" gradually became a separate way of life. Instead of being a stumbling step from childhood into adulthood, it became a culture of its own, with a special language, set of values, program of activities, and philosophy of life. You and your teen friends today have a world all your own, with "teen-age" substitutes for just about everything in adult life. You have your own status system and status symbols. You have your own social merry-go-round. You are the victims of a social change that perhaps nobody could have controlled, but that everybody had better understand.

Let me go one step further: Mr. Manufacturer and Mr. Advertiser are now working on the subteens, *preparing them to be "good" teen-age customers!* Not long ago I visited a large toy store where the latest dolls were on display. Not baby dolls, mind you, nor bride dolls, nor dutiful homemakers. *Teen-age dolls!* —complete with their own wardrobe (at a price), telephone ("Every teen-ager deserves her own phone!"), TV set, sports equipment, cars, and dates. (You pay more for the boy teen-ager, but the girl doll won't be happy without him.) More than 9 million dolls of one series have been sold in the last five years, along with her 60-plus wardrobe items that add another $150 to the original $3 purchase price!

With millions of American subteens "playing teen-ager" with their dolls, it won't be long before they'll all believe that their teen years are made up of nothing but dates, telephones, parties, clothes, and cars. But won't the American manufacturers be happy!

I'm not on an anti-toy crusade. I'm just trying to explain the problem you have to face in your teen years. You live in a society that has twisted the meaning of the word *teen-ager,* a society that consciously or unconsciously is trying to make you an artificial adult. Advertisers know they can play on your emotions and peddle their goods. They gain a profit, you lose a precious personality. You find yourself following the crowd in everything, living for material things instead of real values, and wasting your teen years "playing adult." Then when you graduate from high school and go off to college or that job, you discover that you aren't really prepared for the demands and disappointments of adult life.

It's a vicious circle: children are playing "teen-ager," teens are playing "adult," and when they all become adults, they discover they've already lost the game!

God wants you to live your teen years as a real teen-ager, but this doesn't mean you'll have to forget your teen crowd and crawl in a cave somewhere. Rather, it means that you'll have to follow some basic principles of life, principles that were made particularly for teen-agers and that have been proved a million times over. These principles are illustrated in the lives of six Bible teens—*real teen-agers*—and if you follow their examples, you'll be a real teen-ager, too.

Now, let's meet the first real teen-ager—Joseph, the teen-ager whose dreams came true.

3

Joseph—
Make Your
Dreams Come True!

EVERY TEEN-AGER KNOWS what it is to dream, to live in that magic land of tomorrow where he is always the hero and everybody "lives happily ever after." The characters in that dream may change from day to day, but Mr. Teen never changes and the theme is always the same: success.

There is certainly nothing wrong with dreams. In fact, most great discoveries and inventions started off as dreams. The mistake you can easily make is substituting dreams for honest achievement, making your dreams escapes from reality instead of blueprints for activity. Dreams *alone* never lead to success.

In fact, you had better learn early in your teen career that *dreams without disciplines become nightmares.* And this principle has no better illustration than Joseph, the teen-age dreamer.

The Bible gives us a very full history of Joseph, starting with his seventeenth year. You can divide his exciting life into four stages: the Dreamer, the Worker, the Prisoner, and the Ruler. As you read his story you will discover that God can take a boy's dreams and turn them into reality—*if* the boy submits himself to the disciplines God sends his way.

Genesis 37: And Jacob dwelt in the land wherein his father was a stranger, in the land of Canaan. 2 These are the generations of Jacob. Joseph, being seventeen years old, was feeding the flock with his brethren; and the lad was with the sons of Bilhah, and with the sons of Zilpah, his father's wives: and Joseph brought unto his father their evil report. 3 Now Israel loved Joseph more than all his children, because he was the son of his old age: and he made him a coat of many colours. 4 And when his brethren saw that their father loved him more than all his brethren, they hated him, and could not speak peaceably unto him.

5 And Joseph dreamed a dream, and he told it his brethren: and they hated him yet the more. 6 And he said unto them, Hear, I pray you, this dream which I have dreamed: 7 For, behold, we were binding sheaves in the field, and, lo, my sheaf arose, and also stood upright; and, behold, your sheaves stood round about, and made obeisance to my sheaf. 8 And his brethren said to him, Shalt thou indeed reign over us? or shalt thou indeed have dominion over us? And they hated him yet the more for his dreams, and for his words.

9 And he dreamed yet another dream, and told it his brethen, and said, Behold, I have dreamed a dream more; and, behold, the sun and the moon and the eleven stars made obeisance to me. 10 And he told it to his father, and to his brethren: and his father rebuked him, and said unto him, What is this dream that thou hast dreamed? Shall I and thy mother and thy brethren indeed come to bow down ourselves to thee to the earth? 11 And his brethren envied him; but his father observed the saying.

12 And his brethren went to feed their father's flock in Shechem. 13 And Israel said unto Joseph, Do not thy brethren feed the flock in Shechem? Come, and I

will send thee unto them. And he said to him, Here am I. 14 And he said to him, Go, I pray thee, see whether it be well with thy brethren, and well with the flocks; and bring me word again. So he sent him out of the vale of Hebron, and he came to Shechem.

15 And a certain man found him, and, behold, he was wandering in the field: and the man asked him, saying, What seekest thou? 16 And he said, I seek my brethren: tell me, I pray thee, where they feed their flocks. 17 And the man said, They are departed hence; for I heard them say, Let us go to Dothan. And Joseph went after his brethren, and found them in Dothan. 18 And when they saw him afar off, even before he came near unto them, they conspired against him to slay him. 19 And they said one to another, Behold, this dreamer cometh. 20 Come now therefore, and let us slay him, and cast him into some pit, and we will say, Some evil beast hath devoured him: and we shall see what will become of his dreams. 21 And Reuben heard it, and he delivered him out of their hands; and said, Let us not kill him. 22 And Reuben said unto them, Shed no blood, but cast him into this pit that is in the wilderness, and lay no hand upon him;

that he might rid him out of their hands, to deliver him to his father again.

23 And it came to pass, when Joseph was come unto his brethren, that they stript Joseph out of his coat, his coat of many colours that was on him; 24 And they took him, and cast him into a pit: and the pit was empty, there was no water in it. 25 And they sat down to eat bread: and they lifted up their eyes and looked, and, behold, a company of Ishmeelites came from Gilead with their camels bearing spicery and balm and myrrh, going to carry it down to Egypt. 26 And Judah said unto his brethren, What profit is it if we slay our brother, and conceal his blood? 27 Come, and let us sell him to the Ishmeelites, and let not our hand be upon him; for he is our brother and our flesh. And his brethren were content. 28 Then there passed by Midianites merchantmen; and they drew and lifted up Joseph out of the pit, and sold Joseph to the Ishmeelites for twenty pieces of silver: and they brought Joseph into Egypt.

29 And Reuben returned into the pit; and, behold, Joseph was not in the pit; and he rent his clothes. 30 And he returned unto his brethren, and said, The child is not; and I, whither shall I go?

31 And they took Joseph's coat, and killed a kid of the goats, and dipped the coat in the blood; 32 And they sent the coat of many colours, and they brought it to their father; and said, This have we found: know now whether it be thy son's coat or no. 33 And he knew it, and said, It is my son's coat; an evil beast hath devoured him; Joseph is without doubt rent in pieces. 34 And Jacob rent his clothes, and put sackcloth upon his loins, and mourned for his son many days. 35 And all his sons and all his daughters rose up to comfort him; but he refused to be comforted; and he said, For I will go down into the grave unto my son mourning. Thus his father wept for him. 36 And the Midianites sold him into Egypt unto Potiphar, an officer of Pharaoh's, and captain of the guard.

That's what happened to Joseph the Dreamer. But that's not the end of the story. For the fascinating Bible record of the next three stages in his career, look up Genesis 39:1-20; 39:21—41:13; and 41:14-46.

Quite a story! Imagine what *your* life would be like if God turned *your* teen dreams into reality! Well, if those dreams of yours are in the will of God (as Joseph's were), and if you let God discipline you the way He did

Joseph, then your dreams *will* come true and God will use you for His glory.

It took God thirteen years to make something out of Joseph. Frankly, my sympathies lie with Joseph's brothers when I read what kind of a fellow Joseph was as a teen-ager. He was proud and pampered, for one thing. His old father doted on him and treated him better than the rest of the boys, and that is always a tragic thing for a teen-ager. Joseph did not have to work; instead, his father gave him that beautiful tailored coat that marked Joseph as a ruler, not a servant. Joseph spent most of his time spying on his brothers! In fact, had Joseph stayed home to enjoy Jacob's pampering, he would never have become a success in life. God had some wonderful plans for Joseph; in fact, Joseph was going to rescue the people of Israel and help to make possible the coming of Christ to this world! His dreams of being a ruler would one day come true; but he would never be a success in the hands of Jacob, so God had to step in and go to work.

God used three *disciplines* to make a man out of Joseph; and He wants to use these same disciplines in your life today.

Discipline Number One was *the discipline of service*. God arranged for Joseph to be sold as a slave! He lost his beautiful ruler's coat and wore instead the garments of a slave.

Those hands that never knew toil were now applied to the hardest possible work.

Use your imagination as you picture Joseph, the slave:

A strong Egyptian soldier, obviously an officer, steps up to the slave trader. "I am Potiphar, an officer of Pharaoh's guard; and I need a boy to work in my house."

"Fine, fine!" replies the dealer. "I have a Hebrew lad here—not very strong, but he has possibilities."

They bargain over the price while Joseph stands by helplessly, just beginning to realize that he is no longer a human being; he is now a piece of property!

The captain approaches Joseph. "I am your new master. I am Potiphar, captain of Pharaoh's guard. What is your name?"

Sullenly, Joseph answers, "Joseph."

Slap! The soldier's rough hand tears across Joseph's tender cheek. "Joseph *what?*"

The lad feels his burning cheek and replies, "Joseph, *sir.*"

"That's better! I can see that you don't know what it is to have respect for your elders; and chances are you don't want to work. Well, we can change that!" And giving Joseph a manly shove, he starts back home.

You can see why God had to use the discipline of *service* in Joseph's life, because only through service could He teach Joseph the important lessons he needed to learn if his dreams were to come true. For one thing, Joseph had to learn *humility,* and there is no better way to learn that vital lesson than through service. The teen-ager who has no respect for his elders will never see his dreams come true. Peter puts it this way:

I Peter 5:5-6: Likewise, ye younger, submit yourselves unto the elder. Yea, all of you be subject one to another, and be clothed with humility: for God resisteth the proud, and giveth grace to the humble. Humble yourselves therefore under the mighty hand of God, that he may exalt you in due time.

God had to strip Joseph of his proud garment and clothe him with a slave's uniform that Joseph might learn to be "clothed with humility." The teen-ager who is not willing to work, to take orders, to stoop to do the humble task, will never experience a promotion from God in the future.

It is not easy for today's teens to learn humility. It seems that our whole way of life exalts the teen instead of humbles him! You have your own stores, magazines, radio, and TV shows, and even your own galaxy of "teen-age stars." Juvenile delinquency has become a major problem, with the tragic result that many teens who are really zeros have become heros. If you are not careful, you will get caught in this "hurry-up-and-grow-up" attitude, and you will start "living your own life" and having no respect for your parents or the other adults in your life.

But the other side of the coin is this: if you will use your teen years to be a servant, to learn respect and humility, then when you come out at the other end of the line, you will be ready for adulthood. Your teen dreams will become realities because you allowed God to discipline you.

There is another lesson Joseph had to learn, the lesson of *diligence*. Proverbs 12:24 puts it this way: "The hand of the diligent shall bear rule: but the slothful [*the lazy*] shall be under tribute." Another wise saying from Solomon is Proverbs 22:29: "Seest thou a man diligent in his business? he shall stand before kings. . . ." Diligence simply means faithfulness to do the job right. You do not find too much of this quality in young people today! "Do just enough to get by" is the prevailing attitude; and this explains why many teens never see their dreams come true. Living in a push-button age, with everything done for them, they never know what it is to work, to start the job and do it right to the very finish.

Yes, dreams without disciplines become

nightmares; and the first discipline Joseph experienced was *service*. He had to learn how to work.

The second discipline was *self-control*. We do not have to go into the details of the temptation. Every teen-ager knows that his body is changing, that new drives are coming to the surface, and that it is easy to fall into sexual sins. Some sex problems in your teen life will gradually solve themselves as you understand yourself better and become mature in your thinking. But it is easy to fall into impurity these days, with *sex* being promoted in almost every advertisement, on every newsstand, and in the great entertainment world.

Why did God allow Joseph to be tempted? That he might develop the discipline of self-control, because *the man who cannot control himself will never be able to control others*. God had Joseph slated to be a king; but he had to prove first of all that he could rule the kingdom of his body. The reason great rulers like Samson and Saul lost their crowns was because they could not control themselves. This explains Paul's warning to Christian "athletes":

I Corinthians 9:25-27: And every man that striveth for the mastery is temperate in all things. Now they do it to obtain a corruptible crown; but we an incorruptible. I therefore so run, not as uncertainly; so fight I, not as one that beateth the air: But I keep under my body, and bring it into subjection: lest that by any means, when I have preached to others, I myself should be a castaway.

How did Joseph gain victory over the temptations of the flesh? He obeyed two important rules: (1) ". . . make not provision for the flesh, to fulfil the lusts thereof" (Romans 13:14); and (2) "Flee also youthful lusts . . ." (II Timothy 2:22). Joseph deliberately stayed away from Potiphar's wife; and when she did tempt him, he ran the other way.

The discipline of self-control is important to your future. If you fail to learn control today, you will never know real success tomorrow. Any serious problems in this area should be discussed with your parents, pastor, or physician.

The two disciplines of service and self-control were not enough; God had to use a third discipline, *suffering,* to make a man out of this seventeen-year-old boy.

Nobody enjoys suffering, and a young person especially dislikes being held down, shackled, and confined. Yet God permitted Joseph to remain a prisoner for over two years! He

had a wonderful purpose in view, as Psalm
105:17-19 explains:

He sent a man before them, even Joseph, who was sold for a servant: Whose
feet they hurt with fetters: he was laid in
iron: Until the time that his word came:
the word of the Lord tried him.

For one thing, Joseph learned *patience*
as he waited there in prison, knowing
all the while that he was not guilty. He
also learned to trust the Word of God. Satan
must have said to Joseph, "What ever happened to those dreams? I thought God made
some promises to you?" Faith and patience—
these are only two of the blessings that Joseph
received in prison; but then, every teen-ager
needs to learn faith and patience if he is to
see his dreams come true. "That ye be not
slothful [*lazy*]," says Hebrews 6:12, "but fol-
lowers of them who through faith and patience inherit the promises." And James says,
"Knowing this, that the trying of your faith
worketh patience. But let patience have her
perfect work, that ye may be perfect [*mature*]
and entire, wanting nothing" (1:3-4).

Impatience is certainly a characteristic of
many teens these days. They are impatient to
get out of school, and some drop out even
before they are really prepared for life. They
are impatient to get married, not realizing

that there is a difference between *growing old* and *growing up*. The Christian teen-ager who has experienced the discipline of suffering knows how to trust God's Word and wait. He knows that faith and patience will make his dreams come true.

When you get right down to basics, Joseph had "I" trouble, and the only way God could cure him was through discipline. His worst "I" problem was *importance;* Joseph was proud and God had to make him a servant to teach him humility. His second problem was *impurity;* and it was the discipline of self-control that answered that need. His third problem was *impatience;* the discipline of suffering took care of that.

God took thirteen years to train Joseph and make his dreams come true! And you and I would not be here today had it not been for Joseph. For it was Joseph who saved the Jewish nation in time of famine; and it was through the Jewish nation that God gave us the Bible and the Saviour!

God has a perfect plan for *your* life; but before He can use you, He must discipline you, and this discipline starts in your teen years.

Let God put His dreams into your heart. Then let Him make those dreams come true as you learn the meaning of service, self-control, and suffering.

4

David—
Your Fantastic Future

NO GENERATION IN history has ever faced the fantastic future that you and your teen-age friends face. You have greater opportunities for learning, greater tools for doing things, and, thanks to a tense world situation, a greater motivation to do something constructive. But as the motto of a large insurance company puts it, "The future belongs to those who prepare for it."

The tragedy is that too many teen-agers are sacrificing their fantastic future for a fun-filled present. They have the idea that success is automatic in this modern world, and they little realize that the competition has never been keener or the demands greater. While they are "playing adult," some of their

friends are letting God prepare them for what
He is preparing for them, and they are heading toward that magic goal called *success*.

Before we even define success or discuss the
three principles that lead to it I want you to
read one of the greatest success stories in the
world—the story of David, the shepherd who
became king. I want you to read carefully I
Samuel 16:1—17:54 and II Samuel 5:4-5.

Imagine how today's newspapers (or teen
magazines) would have played up David!
Manufacturers would have paid him plenty to
endorse their sling shots, swords, shields, and
shepherds' crooks! David didn't have too
much to start with, but because he let God
direct his life, he became a great success.

I've used that elusive word "success" several times, so I'd better take time to define it.
Perhaps the best way to do it is to use a story
that Jesus told.

Matthew 25:14-30: 14 For the kingdom of heaven is as a man travelling into
a far country, who called his own
servants, and delivered unto them his
goods. 15 And unto one he gave five talents, to another two, and to another one;
to every man according to his several ability; and straightway took his journey.
16 Then he that had received the five talents went and traded with the same, and

made them other five talents. 17 And likewise he that had received two, he also gained other two. 18 But he that had received one went and digged in the earth, and hid his lord's money. 19 After a long time the lord of those servants cometh, and reckoneth with them. 20 And so he that had received five talents came and brought other five talents, saying, Lord, thou deliveredst unto me five talents: behold, I have gained beside them five talents more. 21 His lord said unto him, Well done, thou good and faithful servant: thou hast been faithful over a few things, I will make thee ruler over many things: enter thou into the joy of thy lord. 22 He also that had received two talents came and said, Lord, thou deliveredst unto me two talents: behold, I have gained two other talents beside them. 23 His lord said unto him, Well done, good and faithful servant; thou hast been faithful over a few things, I will make thee ruler over many things: enter thou into the joy of thy lord. 24 Then he which had received the one talent came and said, Lord, I knew thee that thou art an hard man, reaping where thou hast not sown, and gathering where thou hast not strawed: 25 And I was afraid, and went and hid thy talent in the earth: lo,

there thou hast that is thine. 26 His lord
answered and said unto him, Thou
wicked and slothful servant, thou knew-
est that I reap where I sowed not, and
gather where I have not strawed:
27 Thou oughtest therefore to have put
my money to the exchangers, and then at
my coming I should have received mine
own with usury. 28 Take therefore the
talent from him, and give it unto him
which hath ten talents. 29 For unto every
one that hath shall be given, and he shall
have abundance: but from him that hath
not shall be taken away even that which
he hath. 30 And cast ye the unprofitable
servant into outer darkness: there shall
be weeping and gnashing of teeth.

A successful person, according to Jesus, is
one who makes use of all his God-given opportunities to use his God-given abilities for the
good of others and the glory of God. Read
that definition again and let it become a part
of you. The "talents" in this story were bars
of gold or silver worth a great deal of money.
We use the word "talents" when talking
about playing music, drawing, and other
skills; but Jesus did not mean this at all. The
men in the parable were given talents according to their abilities! In other words, the talents represent *opportunities to use abilities*.

God gives us opportunities to match our abilities, and if we're faithful to use both abilities and opportunities for His glory, then He considers us successful. This is why the two-talent man received the very same reward as the five-talent man: he had been just as faithful.

This story about the talents gives us the three basic principles of success, three principles that can give direction to your teen years and help you prepare for the demands of the future. All three are illustrated in the life of David.

Principle No. 1: We start as servants before God makes us rulers. "Well done, thou good and faithful servant . . . I will make thee ruler. . . ."

God's pattern has always been to start a man at the bottom of the ladder. Joseph, you'll recall, started as a servant in Potiphar's house before God made him a ruler over the land of Egypt. Moses spent forty years as a shepherd before God made him the great leader of Israel. Joshua was Moses' servant before he became Moses' successor. The great Prophet Samuel got his start tending the furniture in the tabernacle!

David knew what it was to start at the bottom. While his older brothers were in the public eye in Saul's army, David was taking care of some sheep. (I wonder what would have happened to David's future if he had insisted, as many teens do today, that his father let him do everything his older brothers did!) David wasn't above doing the chores at home, obeying his father and apparently getting no reward. To put it bluntly, David knew how to serve. He realized that he would never be a success in the nation if he was a failure at home.

I like the way David was faithful to do his job, in spite of problems. When he took his sheep out to pasture that eventful day, he may have thought his brothers were getting a privilege he wasn't getting; yet Samuel bypassed all of them and sent for David! When David took the food to his brothers at the battle, he left the sheep in the care of a friend (I Samuel 17:20) so that his flock would not be scattered. He knew how to obey his father and respect his brothers. He was a teen-age servant, not a celebrity. Even after he left his job at the palace, he went right back to taking care of sheep! Some teens I know would have started a "David and Saul Fan Club" and sold their story to some magazine.

This principle applies to you today. If you resent authority and resist orders, chances are you'll never know real success when you become an adult. Most of the frustrated adults today were pampered children or teens twenty years ago. They never learned how to serve others.

Principle No. 2: We start with few things before God gives us many things. Most modern teens think that life is made up of "things"—TV sets, transistor radios, clothes, cars, and credit cards. They forget that Jesus taught that "a man's life consisteth not in the abundance of the things which he possesseth". (Luke 12:15). God's policy is to see how faithful we are with a few things before He trusts us with many things.

Where is this more clearly seen than in David's life? He started with a few sheep when a teen-ager, and when an adult he received an entire nation! God saw that he was faithful to care for the few sheep, so He made him king over Israel. David killed a lion and a bear in private, so God permitted him to kill a giant in public. David sang to himself while tending the sheep, and today the whole world sings his songs as recorded in the Psalms. As a lad he delivered some food to his brothers at the front; and when an old man, he delivered millions of dollars' worth of materials to Solomon for the building of the temple.

Let me tell you about a British teen-ager of a century ago. He was saved when fifteen and almost immediately began to serve the Lord by passing out tracts to about seventy homes in his neighborhood. When he was sixteen he taught in a Sunday school and began to do some other speaking. At seventeen he was pastoring a small church with about forty members. This grew, and at the age of twenty he was invited to pastor a large London church! He started with only 200 when he took the church, but before long Charles Spurgeon was preaching to the largest crowds in London! He started with a few things, and God gave him charge over many things.

You may dream of making mighty conquests in the future, and there is nothing wrong with that. But make sure you aren't sabotaging your future by neglecting your present. The way you handle high school assignments today will help determine your college career tomorrow. If you're unfaithful in the use of opportunities now, God will never trust you with bigger things later.

Principle No. 3: We start with work before we experience joy.

The philosophy of many teens today is, "Have fun! Act older than you think!" They have the wild idea that their teen years were meant to be a circus with plenty of privileges and no responsibilities. How wrong they are! Sure, there's lots of enjoyment in being a real teen-ager; but fun is only one side of the picture. The other side is work. And most adults know that there's no real enjoyment in life apart from hard work.

This "fun craze" has hit just about every area of life. Check the titles of the books in your local library: *Cooking Can Be Fun! Fun With Figures! Dieting Is Fun!* I once told a convention of young people that I was going to make a million dollars with a new series of text books: *Laughing With Latin, Mirth and Mathematics,* and *History Is Hilarious.* The attitude of many people today is this: If it isn't fun, I'm not interested.

Now, you'd better accept the fact that a real teen-ager can't always have fun. He has to know what it is to work. But the wonderful part of the bargain is that the work you do today is preparing you for the joy tomorrow. Today's toil is really a "postponed pleasure." It's no fun to learn algebra equations or musical scales, but once you've learned them you've opened the door into all kinds of enjoyment. It's no fun for a football team to exercise, diet, and practice, but these activities are actually "postponed pleasures" and investments in an enjoyable future.

David knew how to work, and he knew that employment today results in enjoyment tomorrow. You'll recall that Joseph was a failure at home because his father wouldn't let him work. Once Joseph learned how to work, God gave him all the enjoyment he could contain. And He'll do the same for you.

A real teen-ager, then, has *direction* in his life because he is faithful to work as a servant in a few things. He knows that when the right time comes, God will make him a ruler over many things and will give him happiness.

5

This Way to Failure

SOMETIMES WE LEARN more from failure than from success, so I want to use another of Christ's stories to explain some more about those three principles of success. You perhaps know this story well, but take time now to read again the account of The Prodigal Son.

Luke 15:11-24: 11 And he said, A certain man had two sons: 12 And the younger of them said to his father, Father, give me the portion of goods that falleth to me. And he divided unto them his living. 13 And not many days after the younger son gathered all together, and took his journey into a far country, and there wasted his substance with riotous living. 14 And when he had spent all, there arose a mighty famine in that land; and he began to be in want. 15 And he went and joined himself to a citizen of that country; and he sent him into his fields to feed swine. 16 And he would fain have filled his belly with the husks that the swine did eat: and no man gave unto him. 17 And when he came to himself, he said, How many hired servants of my father's have bread enough and to spare, and I perish with hunger! 18 I will arise and go to my father, and will say unto him, Father, I have sinned against heaven, and before thee, 19 And am no more worthy to be called thy son: make me as one of thy hired servants. 20 And he arose, and came to his father. But when he was yet a great way off, his father saw him, and had compassion, and ran, and fell on his neck, and kissed him. 21 And the son said unto him, Father, I have sinned against heaven, and in thy sight, and am no more worthy to be called thy son. 22 But the father said to his servants, Bring forth the best robe, and put it on him; and put a ring on his hand, and shoes on his feet: 23 And bring hither the fatted calf, and kill it; and let us eat, and be merry: 24 For this my son was dead, and is alive again, he was lost, and is found. And they began to be merry.

If David illustrates God's principles for success, then the Prodigal pictures the world's principles for success. David and the Prodigal stand for two opposite philosophies of life, and it's important that you know the difference.

The Prodigal started with many things and ended with nothing! Like some teens today, he wanted to get all he could and enjoy it while he was young. He was indifferent to his father's pleas; he wanted "things" and he wanted them right now. "Father, give me!" is, unfortunately, the motto of many young people these days. They little realize that the person who starts off with "Give me!" ends up saying "Forgive me!"

The Prodigal wanted to live, and he thought that life meant possessing things and having a lot of friends. He knew a great deal about prices but nothing about values. He thought that success was measured in dollar signs. He wanted all the things that money could buy, not knowing that the things money can buy are worthless without the things money can't buy. After all, what good is a $100,000 house if you don't have a home? Or a $10,000 wardrobe if you have a sick body? Or a $5,000 diamond ring if there is no lasting love?

You can be sure that the teen-ager who grasps for things will never really be rich. "Playing adult" usually includes accumulating a lot of things—teen-age status symbols that never really satisfy the heart. Don't forget the rich farmer who one night heard God say, "Thou fool, this night thy soul shall be required of thee: then whose shall those things be, which thou hast provided?" (Luke 12:20).

The Prodigal started as a ruler, and ended up a servant! What a faithful gang of friends he had—until his money ran out! The world promised him success, but he ended up with the pigs! He wanted to live "high on the hog" and ended living lower than the hogs!

Disobedience to God's principles always leads to failure and sorrow. You may think you know some short cut to success, but that short cut always turns out to be the most expensive road—and detours are always rough! Be willing to wait. Be a servant today and your opportunity will come; and when it does come, you'll be prepared for it.

The Prodigal started with joy and ended with sorrow. This young man was on the "fun kick" when he left home, but the fun didn't last very long. When a person lives on substitutes and those substitutes run out, nothing is left but disappointment and sorrow. He thought that real joy came from money, parties, sin, and liberty; he discovered that sin promises happiness but always delivers tragedy.

I can imagine the boy saying to his father, "It's no fun staying at home! I'm going to leave home and have a good time in life." But when he "came to himself" he realized that there was no place like home. The trouble wasn't in his home but in his heart.

The real teen-ager follows David's philosophy and is willing to let God prepare him for his fantastic future. The artificial adult, the teen-ager who is "playing adult," has adopted the Prodigal's philosophy and wants everything right now.

Nobody has to tell you which of these two philosophies is the better.

Which one have *you* chosen?

6

Daniel—
Transformer or Conformer?

THE TWO REAL teen-agers we've met so far have helped you understand, I hope, the *disciplines* and *directions* needed for your teen years. You may be saying to yourself at this point, "This is for me! I'm going to be another Joseph or David!" I'm happy for your ambitions, but I have to warn you: it takes more than Joseph's three disciplines and David's three directions for success to be a real teen-ager. You also need Daniel, that Jewish teen-age refugee who eventually helped rule an empire.

You see, Daniel illustrates the *decisions* necessary to your success as a teen-ager.

Daniel 1:1-21: In the third year of the reign of Jehoiakim king of Judah came Nebuchadnezzar king of Babylon unto Jerusalem, and besieged it. 2 And the Lord gave Jehoiakim king of Judah into his hand, with part of the vessels of the house of God: which he carried into the land of Shinar to the house of his god; and he brought the vessels into the treasure house of his god.

3 And the king spake unto Ashpenaz the master of his eunuchs, that he should bring certain of the children of Israel, and of the king's seed, and of the princes; 4 Children in whom was no blemish, but well favoured, and skilful in all wisdom, and cunning in knowledge, and understanding science, and such as had ability in them to stand in the king's palace, and whom they might teach the learning and the tongue of the Chaldeans. 5 And the king appointed them a daily provision of the king's meat, and of the wine which he drank: so nourishing them three years, that at the end thereof they might stand before the king. 6 Now among these were of the children of Judah, Daniel, Hananiah, Mishael, and Azariah: 7 Unto whom the prince of the eunuchs gave names: for he gave unto Daniel the name of Belteshazzar, and to Hananiah, of Shadrach; and

to Mishael, of Meshach; and to Azariah, of Abednego.

8 But Daniel purposed in his heart that he would not defile himself with the portion of the king's meat, nor with the wine which he drank: therefore he requested of the prince of the eunuchs that he might not defile himself. 9 Now God had brought Daniel into favour and tender love with the prince of the eunuchs. 10 And the prince of the eunuchs said unto Daniel, I fear my lord the king, who hath appointed your meat and your drink: for why should he see your faces worse liking than the children which are of your sort? then shall ye make me endanger my head to the king. 11 Then said Daniel to Melzar, whom the prince of the eunuchs had set over Daniel, Hananiah, Mishael, and Azariah, 12 Prove thy servants, I beseech thee, ten days; and let them give us pulse to eat, and water to drink. 13 Then let our countenances be looked upon before thee, and the countenance of the children that eat of the portion of the king's meat: and as thou seest, deal with thy servants. 14 So he consented to them in this matter, and proved them ten days. 15 And at the end of ten days their countenances

appeared fairer and fatter in flesh than all the children which did eat the portion of the king's meat. 16 Thus Melzar took away the portion of their meat, and the wine that they should drink; and gave them pulse.

17 As for these four children, God gave them knowledge and skill in all learning and wisdom: and Daniel had understanding in all visions and dreams. 18 Now at the end of the days that the king had said he should bring them in, then the prince of the eunuchs brought them in before Nebuchadnezzar. 19 And the king communed with them; and among them all was found none like Daniel, Hananiah, Mishael, and Azariah: therefore stood they before the king. 20 And in all matters of wisdom and understanding, that the king inquired of them, he found them ten times better than all the magicians and astrologers that were in all his realm. 21 And Daniel continued even unto the first year of king Cyrus.

The first decision Daniel had to make was whether he was going to be a *conformer* or a *transformer*. The leaders in Babylon did their best to make Daniel conform. They took him from Jerusalem to Babylon and gave him a new home, a new name, new ideas, a new diet, a new language, and even new gods! They wanted to "brainwash" him and make him one of their puppets. To be sure, had Daniel given in he could have had status and security for years to come; but he would have missed God's great purpose for his life.

Your situation today isn't much different from Daniel's. As a Christian, your "citizenship is in heaven" (Philippians 3:20, where "conversation" really means "citizenship") but you're forced to live in this present world until such time as God calls you home. But this world is no friend to Christ or Christians and would like to "brainwash" you and force you to conform. Unfortunately, many Christian teens *do* conform and consequently miss the best God has for them.

This is a good time to make an important distinction between the conformer and transformer. A conformer is a person whose life is controlled by pressures from without; a transformer is a person whose life is controlled by power from within. Daniel had to decide (as you do) whether he was going to let Babylon change him, or whether he was going to change Babylon.

Daniel could have argued his way into being a conformer. Like some teens today, he could have given several excuses (he might have called them "reasons") for going along with the pressures being applied. "Everybody else is doing it!" would have sounded like a valid reason, because just about everybody else *was* doing it! It appears that Daniel and his three teen-age friends were the only ones willing to stand their ground.

Of course, Daniel could have said, "The king commanded it, so I'd better obey." (Several centuries later, the apostles would say, "We ought to obey God rather than men"— Acts 5:29). Or, Daniel might have argued, "We can obey outwardly, but keep our true faith inwardly." They could have enlisted in a "secret service" and perhaps worked underground, except that God has no secret service and compromise with the enemy is the first step toward defeat.

You and I have both heard (and perhaps used) these and many more excuses for conforming to the world around us and avoiding the shame and suffering that often comes to a transformer. From a human point of view, Daniel and his three friends were fools for refusing the king's offers. What a great future he had planned for them—free education, fame, security, status, wealth! What more could a teen-ager want?

Daniel chose to be a transformer, and I hope you'll make the same decision. In order to understand what it means to be a transformer, we must discover the pressures around you that can make you conform, and then the power God has for you to use in overcoming these pressures.

I'm sure that many times you've heard people talk about "the world" or "worldly Christians." Or, perhaps you've read verses like these in your Bible:

1 John 2:15-17: 15 Love not the world, neither the things that are in the world. If any man love the world, the love of the Father is not in him. 16 For all that is in the world, the lust of the flesh, and the lust of the eyes, and the pride of life, is not of the Father, but is of the world. 17 And the world passeth away, and the lust thereof; but he that doeth the will of God abideth for ever.

You may have asked yourself, "What in the world is 'the world'?" I want to answer that question right now.

The Bible uses the word *world* in at least three ways. It speaks of the *material world*: "God that made the world and all things therein . . ." (Acts 17:24); a second meaning is the *human world*: "For God so loved the world . . ." (John 3:16); but the Bible also speaks of *an invisible system, controlled by Satan, that opposes the work of Christ*—"the world." The word *world* is used in this way in I John 2:15-17, Romans 12:2, John 17:16, and in many other places. When the Bible warns you, "Love not the world!" or "Be not conformed to the world!" it has this invisible system in mind.

Let me illustrate. Have you ever turned on your radio or TV to hear the news and heard the announcer say, "And now the news from the world of sports"? What did he mean by "the world of sports"? Did he refer to a special planet populated only by athletes, umpires, and spectators? Of course not! "The world of sports" is a phrase that includes all the people, places, events, plans, and philosophies that relate to sports. "The world of sports" includes things visible and invisible, but things real and powerful nonetheless.

All around you every single day is this invisible system that the Bible calls *the world*. As a Christian, you are *in* the physical and human world, but *not in* the world-system that is out to oppose Christ.

Perhaps a diagram will make all this clear. When you came into this human world, you brought with you a body, mind, and will. All of your abilities, appetites, and achievements were wrapped up in your body, mind, and will. When you became a Christian, the Holy Spirit of God moved into your life and made your body His temple (I Corinthians 6:19-20); so we can diagram a Christian like this:

Now, all around you is the Satanic world-system that the Bible calls *the world*. Daniel had it around him in Babylon, and you have it in Chicago, Los Angeles, Grove Junction or wherever you are. So, let's add *the world* to our diagram:

You'll remember that I John 2:16 identifies three "pressures" that the world exerts against you all the time, pressures that can make you conform to the world and thereby lose your testimony as a Christian. These pressures work on your body ("the lust, or appetite, of the flesh"), your mind ("the appetite of the eyes"), and your will ("the pride of life"). Let's add these pressures to our diagram:

Go back to Daniel in Babylon and you'll have some idea of how these pressures work. He faced pressure against his body as the king's servants offered him a new diet and tempted him with things unlawful for a Jew to eat. The new ideas and "wisdom" that they taught him exerted pressure against his mind —not unlike modern "brainwashing." And the wonderful offers of money and position worked on his will and would have conquered him. Had Daniel given in to these subtle pressures, he would have become a conformer, lost his testimony and power, and never gone down in history as a real teen-ager.

But he didn't give in! Daniel knew the secret of being a transformer, and he used the divine power within him to overcome the pressures without. What is that secret?

> *Romans 12:1-2:* I beseech you therefore, brethren, by the mercies of God, that ye present your bodies a living sacrifice, holy, acceptable unto God, which is your reasonable service. 2 And be not conformed to this world: but be ye transformed by the renewing of your mind, that ye may prove what is that good, and acceptable, and perfect, will of God.

Note those two important words, *conformed* and *transformed*. Paul tells us here that any Christian can be a transformer by surrendering himself to God—body, mind, and will. Here it is:

> ". . . present your *bodies* a living sacrifice"
> ". . . the renewing of your *minds*."
> ". . . prove that good, acceptable, and perfect, *will* of God."

That's the meaning of dedication: daily surrendering of body, mind, and will to God for Him to control and use.

Here's how it works. You wake up in the morning and the very first thing you do is yield your body, mind, and will to God. This is an act of faith, a "spiritual sacrifice" similar to the burnt offering the Jewish priests placed on the altar early each morning. Then you get up and open your Bible, allowing the Word of God to renew your mind. This means reading the Word, understanding it, and making it a part of your life. The next step is prayer, and here you present to God your praise and petitions with a yielded will. "Not my will, but Thine be done!" When you have done this, you are a dedicated teenager and the indwelling Holy Spirit is in control. (If this is merely a routine, of course, then there is no dedication. It has to come from the heart.)

No sooner do you step out of your room than the world starts putting pressure on you. Perhaps it exerts pressure against your body, trying to get you to live for your body or use your body as the people of the world do. When you sense that pressure at work, simply say, "Father, take over my body! It's yielded to Thy control!" And the Spirit on the inside counteracts the pressure on the outside— and you get the victory!

Perhaps the pressure is exerted against your mind, and you're tempted to think the way the world thinks—"Go ahead and cheat on the exam! You'll get away with it. Everybody does." When you turn your mind over to God by faith, then the power on the inside (the Holy Spirit) counteracts the pressure on the outside, and you overcome that temptation.

Perhaps you're walking down the corridor at school and somebody races by, knocking you into the wall and scattering your books all over the place. That proud will of yours (and we all have one!) immediately reacts, and the pressure from the world goes to work, tempting you to lose your temper and tell somebody what you think. Instead, you ask the Spirit to take over, and His power from within counteracts that pressure from without, and you smile and get the victory—and give a better testimony.

This if the simple secret of being a transformer instead of a conformer. Because Daniel surrendered body, mind, and will to God, and spent time daily in the Word of God and prayer (see Daniel 6:1-11 and 9:2), he was able to live a godly life in a very ungodly nation. Because he fixed his heart on God and not on the world, God honored him and made him a real success in every way (see Daniel 1:8-20).

There's one more matter I want to discuss before we leave Daniel and move into the New Testament to meet another real teen-ager, and that's the subject of *worldliness*. What is worldliness? How can you tell when these pressures are at work in your life? How can a Christian teen-ager tell right from wrong when so many Christians disagree on these matters? I'll take these questions up in the next chapter, but I'd suggest you visit Daniel again and review this chapter carefully.

7

How Far Can a Teen-ager Go?

HE HAD A determined look on his face and he was heading right for me! I had just finished speaking to a youth conference, and apparently something I had said had aroused either his interest or his anger.

"This business about conforming to the world is all well and good," he exploded, without even introducing himself, "but the world *I* live in isn't black and white. It's various shades of gray, and sometimes I don't really know what's right and what's wrong!"

"That's interesting," I replied, "because people in Bible days faced the same problem. Have you ever read Paul's First Letter to the Christians at Corinth?"

"A little," he answered. "But those people

didn't know anything about TV or school plays or any of the other things that bother me and my Christian friends." Then he asked the question I had heard scores of teens ask across the country: "Just how far can a Christian teen-ager go?"

We sat down with our Bibles, opened to I Corinthians, and discovered the answer to that question. Put yourself in that boy's place and let me show you how the Bible solves this typical teen problem.

To begin with, the Bible deals with *principles,* not rules and regulations. Of course, there are specific rules and warnings in the Bible; but when it comes to the area of questionable things, the Bible lays down principles instead. A principle is something that applies and works regardless of the time or situation, while a specific rule usually applies to a specific situation. Some sins, of course, can be named specifically: it's *always* wrong to lie, steal, lose your temper, etc. You will find these sins in *every* culture and civilization; but matters like TV, movies, school events, dancing, etc., are relatively modern and the Bible doesn't mention them. Instead, God gives us basic principles, or tests, that apply just as effectively today as they did in Corinth or Rome twenty centuries ago.

If you had been a Christian teen-ager in Corinth, for example, you would have faced the problem of food being offered to idols (I Corinthians 8). We all know that an idol is not a real god, and that food dedicated to an idol is not contaminated. But there were some Christians at Corinth who were offended when their Christian friends ate meat that had been offered to idols when it was served to them in their friends' houses. (In fact, the cheapest meat in town came from the temple sacrifices!)

Instead of saying, "Thou shalt not!" the Apostle Paul gave four spiritual principles (or tests) for the believers to apply to their own lives. These four principles answer the question, "How far can a Christian go?"

1. *Will this lead to freedom or slavery?* Read I Corinthians 6:12.

All things are lawful unto me, but all things are not expedient [profitable]: all things are lawful for me, but I will not be brought under the power of any.

The real issue, then, is not whether a thing is lawful or even approved; the issue is, *Will it make a slave out of me?* Anything that gets control over a Christian is wrong, even if others think it is right. Take sports, for example. I have seen wonderful Christian fellows go downhill spiritually after getting involved with school athletics. Not that playing football or baseball is a sin. In fact, participation in school sports can be a real testimony—*provided* the Lord comes first. But when a Christian teen-ager's mind is so filled with winning the game that he has no thought for the Bible, prayer, witnessing, church, or other spiritual matters, then he has become a slave —and this is sin. The same principle applies to dating: if a fellow or girl becomes so important that Christ loses His place of pre-eminence, then even Christians dating other Christians and going to Christian places can be wrong.

2. *Is this thing making me a stumbling block or a stepping stone?* Read I Corinthians 8:9:

> But take heed lest by any means this liberty of yours become a stumblingblock to them that are weak.

"You and I both know," writes Paul, in other words, "that eating dedicated meat in a heathen temple is not going to make you spiritually weak. But suppose a weaker Christian sees you there, and his own conscience is offended? He will use you as an excuse to do things that used to bother him, and if he ends up in sin, you are to blame!" The real issue is not what these questionable practices will do to *you* personally, but *what they will do to those who watch you.* After all, you are the best Christian somebody knows! It is far better to sacrifice the questionable thing and be the best example possible than to risk the danger of making some other teen-ager stumble into sin.

3. *Will it build me up or tear me down?* Read I Corinthians 10:23 (the word "edify" in this verse means "to build up"):

> All things are lawful for me, but all things are not expedient: all things are lawful for me, but all things edify not.

Life is too short to be tearing yourself down physically, mentally, emotionally, or spiritually! You have only one body; take care of it! Your Uncle Pete may be able to read certain magazines, but if you read them, they would tear you down. If you detect *anything* in your life—even a "good" thing—that dulls your spiritual appetite or makes it easy to sin, then get rid of it in a hurry.

Now, this doesn't mean that you should experiment with sin. You don't have to rob a bank or cheat on an exam to discover that stealing will tear you down. You don't have to walk in the back door of the local tavern to know that alcohol is a destroyer. These practices are pretty clearly covered in the Bible as well as in the experience of mature people down through the years. But when it comes to the questionable things that even some Christians disagree on, you'll have to test them for yourself—honestly and prayerfully—to see whether they build you up or tear you down.

4. *Will this simply please me, or will it glorify God?* Read I Corinthians 10:31:

> Whether therefore ye eat, or drink, or whatsoever ye do, do all to the glory of God.

As a Christian, your privilege—and responsibility—is to use your body to *glorify* God and to *magnify* God. ". . . therefore glorify God in your body . . . ," commands I Corinthians 6:20; and Paul says in Philippians 1:20 that he wants Christ to be "magnified" in his body, "whether it be by life or by death." If you practice something that glorifies *you* or magnifies *you* in the eyes of your friends, but minimizes (or even disgraces) your Saviour, then that practice is wrong. In fact, it's just plain selfish!

These are four tests you can use every day to decide what is right and wrong in this area of questionable things. The only requirement is that you be perfectly honest in your dealings with God. "Let every man be fully persuaded in his own mind" (Romans 14:5). It would pay you to read all of Romans 14 because it deals in detail with this problem.

This much is certain: the Christian teenager who honestly follows these principles, and who is anxious to please Christ in everything, will find himself walking in the sunlight of God's best instead of the shadows of compromise.

8

Mary—
You Can Be a Miracle!

"WHY IN THE world did you do it?" the juvenile court judge asked four teen-agers accused of breaking into a garage and beating up an old watchman—all for $1.76!

"There was nothin' else to do," the ringleader answered. "We just got bored and wanted something to do. That's all."

Boredom—nothing to do—is a real problem with many teen-agers. (Not that school work and home responsibilities aren't enough to keep you busy!) Life can become (as one girl explained to me) "just plain ordinary." And when life gets ordinary, you start looking for excitement—cars, dates, crowds, entertainment, and (too often) sin.

Life could have been ordinary for Mary,

the teen-age girl God chose to become the mother of Jesus. (That's right—I said *teen-age* girl. Jewish girls married in their teens in those days, and most authorities I've consulted agree that Mary was probably about fifteen or sixteen when she gave birth to Jesus.) She lived in the village of Nazareth, not the big city of Jerusalem. Nazareth was located on a main highway, so she undoubtedly saw the Roman legions marching past and the merchants with their wares. But Nazareth didn't have too savory a reputation. "Can there any good thing come out of Nazareth?" Nathanael asked Philip (John 1:46). Mary could have said, "Life is dull here! I'm going to Jerusalem or Rome and enjoy myself!" If she had, she would have become the prodigal daughter instead of the honored mother of Jesus!

Yet Mary was the happiest girl in Nazareth! She may not have had a large wardrobe, a bank account, or any of the scores of trinkets that many teens think they cannot do without; but she was nevertheless a joyful teen-ager. Just read the record and notice how many times she talks about *joy*.

Luke 1:26-56: 26 And in the sixth month the angel Gabriel was sent from God unto a city of Galilee, named Nazareth. 27 To a virgin espoused to a man whose name was Joseph, of the house of David; and the virgin's name was Mary. 28 And the angel came in unto her, and said, Hail, thou that art highly favoured, the Lord is with thee: blessed art thou among women. 29 And when she saw him, she was troubled at his saying, and cast in her mind what manner of salutation this should be. 30 And the angel said unto her, Fear not, Mary: for thou hast found favour with God. 31 And, behold, thou shalt conceive in thy womb, and bring forth a son, and shalt call his name JESUS. 32 He shall be great, and shall be called the Son of the Highest: and the Lord God shall give him the throne of his father David: 33 And he shall reign over the house of Jacob for ever; and of his kingdom there shall be no end. 34 Then said Mary unto the angel, How shall this be, seeing I know not a man? 35 And the angel answered and said unto her, The Holy Ghost shall come upon thee, and the power of the Highest shall overshadow thee; therefore also that holy thing which shall be born of thee shall be called the Son of God. 36 And, behold, thy cousin Elisabeth, she hath also conceived a son in her old age: and this is the sixth month with her, who was called barren. 37 For with God nothing shall be impossible. 38 And Mary said, Behold the handmaid of the Lord; be it unto me according to thy word. And the angel departed from her. 39 And Mary arose in those days, and went into the hill country with haste, into a city of Juda; 40 And entered into the house of Zacharias, and saluted Elisabeth. 41 And it came to pass, that, when Elisabeth heard the salutation of Mary, the babe leaped in her womb; and Elisabeth was filled with the Holy Ghost. 42 And she spake out with a loud voice, and said, Blessed art thou among women, and blessed is the fruit of thy womb. 43 And whence is this to me, that the mother of my Lord should come to me? 44 For, lo, as soon as the voice of thy salutation sounded in mine ears, the babe leaped in my womb for joy. 45 And blessed is she that believed: for there shall be a performance of those things which were told her from the Lord. 46 And Mary said, My soul doth magnify the Lord. 47 And my spirit hath rejoiced in God my Saviour. 48 For he hath regarded the low estate of his handmaiden: for, behold, from henceforth all generations shall call me blessed. 49 For he that is mighty hath done to me great things; and holy is his name. 50 And his mercy is on them that fear him from generation to generation. 51 He hath shewed strength with his arm; he hath scattered the proud in the imagination of their hearts. 52 He hath put down the mighty from their seats, and exalted them of low degree. 53 He hath filled the hungry with good things; and the rich he hath sent empty away. 54 He hath holpen his servant Israel, in remembrance of his mercy; 55 As he spake to our fathers, to Abraham, and to his seed for ever. 56 And Mary abode with her about three months, and returned to her own house.

Exciting, isn't it! *God made Mary's life into a miracle!* Her joy wasn't simply a passing pleasure or a temporary thrill; it was something lasting and satisfying *because it was on the inside.* If you are depending on outside sources of joy, then you will always be disappointed. But if you let Christ work on the inside, you will experience the miracle-joy that Mary knew—and life won't be ordinary any longer!

There were four sources of joy in Mary's life.

The joy of salvation: Mary was a *saved* teenager, and this is where real joy begins. The first miracle in your life must be the miracle of salvation, of putting your faith in Jesus

Christ. And this is just the "beginning of miracles"!

Did Mary *need* to be saved? Of course she did! You noticed that she calls God her "Saviour" in verse 47; and Dr. Luke traces her family all the way back to *Adam* (3:38). That's the whole trouble: all of us are children of Adam, and that makes us sinners. Mary wasn't saved because she was singled out to be the channel through whom Christ would come into the world. No, she was saved because she trusted God's promise.

How is *any* sinner saved? Ephesians 2:8-9 explains how:

> For by *grace* are ye saved through faith; and that not of yourselves: it is the gift of God: Not of works, lest any man should boast.

By grace, through faith—it's that simple! That is the way Mary was saved. The angel said to her, "Grace, thou that art highly graced!" And Elisabeth said of Mary, "Happy is she that *believed*." Grace and faith are the secrets of the miracle of salvation, the miracle that brings real joy.

Have you experienced this miracle? If not, why not believe God's promise and open your heart to Him? Then you will know the same joy that Mary knew: the joy of sins forgiven, the joy of being a child in God's family forever and forever.

There was a second joy that Mary had—

The joy of surrender: "Behold the handmaid [bondslave] of the Lord," said Mary, "be it unto me according to thy word." This is surrender, a yielding of body, mind, and will to the control of God.

This surrender was a costly thing to Mary. After all, she was going to bear a Baby and she was not yet married. Of course, she was engaged to Joseph, and he willingly married her after God explained His plan to him (Matthew 1:18-25); but people would still talk, and it may be that John 8:41 reflects the attitude people had toward Christ's birth: "Then said they to him, We be not born of fornication. . . ." In spite of the gossip and misunderstanding, Mary surrendered herself to the Lord for Him to use her as He planned.

There is no reason for you to be afraid of surrender. In fact, there will be no real joy in your life until you give your all to Christ. You don't find Mary complaining, do you? Of course not! You find her singing! First the sacrifice, then the song. At least that's the way you find it in II Chronicles 29:27: "And when the burnt offering began, the song of the Lord began also. . . ." Perhaps the reason your life has been "ordinary" and joyless is because you have not yet surrendered to Christ.

Mary illustrates perfectly what a surrendered Christian does. First of all, *she lived by the Bible:* ". . . be it unto me according to thy word." Mary was God's "handmaid," and that title refers to the lowliest kind of a servant. She had no will of her own; God's will, as revealed in God's Word, controlled her life. Then, *she lived to magnify Christ:* "My soul doth magnify the Lord" she sang. As far as your friends are concerned, Christ is not very important: He is small in comparison to other people in their lives, and He seems so far away. You and I must be magnifiers and make Christ important and near.

The third joy in Mary's life was—

The joy of the Scriptures: The amazing thing about her song (Luke 1:46-55) is that it is filled with quotations from the Old Testament—and Mary did not own a Bible! The common people of Jesus' day didn't have copies of the Old Testament; they *heard* it read daily at the synagogue. Mary had never gone through a Bible Memory Course at a youth camp, but she knew the Word of God and was able to quote it. In fact, her song contains quotations from the Law, the Prophets, and the Psalms.

The happiest teens I know are the ones who know the Word of God. You see, Satan's chief weapon is a lie; Jesus makes it very clear in John 8:44 that you can never trust the devil: ". . . for he is a liar, and the father of it." If Satan can get you to believe one of his lies he will have you in his hands. After all, Eve believed one of his lies (Genesis 3) and her disobedience, along with Adam's, brought ruin to the whole race! But the Christian who knows God's truth can answer the devil's lies and go on in victory. That's what Jesus did when Satan tempted Him (Luke 4:1-13); His "It is written!" defeated Satan at every turn.

The Bible is the best Book; and the best place for it is in your heart. "Thy word have I hid in mine heart, that I might not sin against thee" (Psalm 119:11). Mary was a joyful teen-ager because she hid the Word in her heart and honored the Word in her life. The teen-ager who spends time *daily* in the Word is going to recognize the devil's lies, avoid the devil's snares, and enjoy Christ's best in his life.

I said that Mary's song was really composed of many quotations from the Old Testament. She did what the Psalmist had done in Psalm 119:54: "Thy statutes have been my songs in the house of my pilgrimage." The Bible was not a burden to Mary; it was a blessing. Even God's laws were a joy to her! This is the real test of dedication: *Do I enjoy studying and obeying the Word of God?* If Mary could learn much of the Word without owning a Bible, how much more ought you and I to learn?

Behind the three joys we have already mentioned is the fourth joy—

The joy of the Spirit: Don't be afraid of the Holy Spirit! If you are a Christian, the Holy Spirit lives within you and has made your body His temple. His responsibility is to make Christ real to you and to help you make Christ real to your unsaved friends. When Christ was on earth physically, He was limited by time and space; now that He has gone back to heaven and sent the Holy Spirit as His "Substitute," He can work in and through Christians all over the world. When Paul wrote in Galatians 2:20, "Christ liveth in me," he was referring to the presence and power of the Spirit in his life.

It was the Holy Spirit who overshadowed Mary and made her the mother of Christ (Luke 1:35). It was the Spirit who brought the Word to her mind and gave her a song to sing. There is simply no substitute for the joy of the Spirit! Your unsaved friends may enjoy the "pleasures of sin for a season" (Hebrews 11:25) as they live for their bodies and fleshly appetites; but you may enjoy the happiness of heaven through the Holy Spirit within. "Now the God of hope fill you with all joy and peace in believing, that ye may abound in hope, through the power of the Holy Ghost," says Romans 15:13.

What are the evidences that the Holy Spirit is working in your life? Paul lists them in Ephesians 5:18-21:

> . . . but be filled with the Spirit; Speaking to yourselves in psalms and hymns and spiritual songs, singing and making melody in your heart to the Lord; Giving thanks always for all things unto God and the Father in the name of our Lord Jesus Christ; Submitting yourselves one to another in the fears of God.

The three evidences of the Spirit's control are: the believer is *joyful, thankful,* and *submissive.* Mary was all three! Now, read Colossians 3:16-17:

> Let the word of Christ dwell in you richly in all wisdom; teaching and admonishing one another in psalms and hymns and spiritual songs, singing with grace in your hearts to the Lord. And whatsoever ye do in word or deed, do all in the name of the Lord Jesus, giving thanks to God and the Father by him. Wives, submit yourselves. . . .

Do you see the parallel? When you are filled with the Spirit you know it because you are joyful, thankful, and submissive. When you are filled with the Word of God you are joyful, thankful, and submissive! *To be filled with the Spirit means to be controlled by the Word!* And because Mary knew the Word, hid it in her heart, and obeyed it, the Spirit was able to fill her and give her overflowing joy!

In the next chapter I'm going to explain further how the Holy Spirit works in your life; but now is a good time to ask yourself: "Have I let God make *me* into a miracle, or is life ordinary and boring?" Have you experienced the joy of salvation? Have you surrendered your body, mind, and will to God, for Him to use for His glory? Do you spend time with your Bible, hiding it in your heart? If so, the Spirit can fill you and transform an ordinary teen-ager into a living miracle!

9

The Ins and Outs
of the Christian Life

DON'T SKIP THIS chapter! And don't argue that the doctrine of the Spirit is for old people and not teen-agers! You'll recall that Joseph knew the work of the Spirit in his life, and so did David. The Spirit gave Daniel amazing wisdom in Babylon, and He worked miracles in the life of Mary. If the Spirit could use those Bible teens, why can't He use you?

You ought to memorize Philippians 2:12-13:

> . . . work out your own salvation with fear and trembling. For it is God which worketh in you both to will and to do of his good pleasure.

Of course, Paul is not saying, "Work *for* your own salvation." Nobody can work *for* salvation; Christ finished that work on the cross. Salvation does not mean that Christ made the down payment and we keep up the installments by our own works! "Work out your own salvation" means "Fulfill in your Christian life the purpose for which you were saved." In Ephesians 2:10, Paul says:

For we are his workmanship, created in Christ Jesus unto good works, which God hath before ordained that we should walk in them.

In short, God has a perfect blueprint for your life, a plan that will bring you the most happiness and Him the most glory. But this plan isn't something you and I try to "work out" on our own; it's something we work out *as God works in us*. That's why I've entitled this chapter "The Ins and Outs of the Christian Life." I want to get across a simple but important principle: *God cannot work through you until first He works in you*. He works in; we work out.

The big question at this point is: *How* does God work in you? And the answer is: Through His Holy Spirit. But that raises another question: How does the Holy Spirit work in you? That's the question I want to answer now.

The Holy Spirit never works in a vacuum; He always uses *means* to do His work in your life. If you were to lock yourself in your room and plead with the Spirit to make your life a miracle—all the while ignoring the *means* that He uses—you would be asking for a nervous breakdown or a Satanic substitute for real spirituality. (Don't forget that the devil is an imitator, and that getting you to live on shallow emotions and false feelings is one of his most effective stratagems. When the feeling wears out, your dedication is gone, and you're discouraged.)

There are three special "tools" that the Spirit wants to use in your life: prayer, the Bible, and suffering. Let's begin with *prayer*. Ephesians 3:16-21 makes it clear that the power of the indwelling Spirit goes to work in your life when you pray:

16 That he would grant you, according to the riches of his glory, to be strengthened with might by his Spirit in the inner man; 17 That Christ may dwell in your hearts by faith; that ye, being rooted and grounded in love, 18 May be able to comprehend with all saints what is the breadth, and length, and depth, and height; 19 And to know the love of

Christ, which passeth knowledge, that ye might be filled with all the fulness of God. 20 Now unto him that is able to do exceeding abundantly above all that we ask or think, according to the power that worketh in us, 21 Unto him be glory in the church by Christ Jesus throughout all ages, world without end. Amen.

That's a long and complicated paragraph, but the main message is clear. When you pray in faith and love, the Spirit empowers the inner man and God goes to work *in* your life and *through* your life.

Have you ever noticed that the people God uses are people who pray? Even as a teen-ager, Daniel was a believer who practiced daily prayer, a habit he continued all his life (Daniel 6:10-11). David knew how to pray; in fact, many of the Psalms are prayers he lifted to God in times of trouble and triumph. Jesus prayed and taught His disciples to pray. The Christian who prays daily is inviting the Spirit to work in his life.

Of course, praying can't be a hit-or-miss affair; it has to be a part of your life, and it must come from your heart. A hurried prayer after a hurried reading of the Bible is a mere routine, and an *empty* routine at that. Real praying has to be cultivated, just like real friendship. Rushing into God's presence, racing through a prayer list, and rushing out again is a dangerous waste of time—dangerous because it's a subtle substitute for the real thing. Real prayer involves: (1) *adoration,* or the worship of God; (2) *appreciation,* thanking God for His mercies; (3) *dedication,* giving yourself to Him for whatever He wills; and (4) *supplication,* asking Him for the things you need and for the things others need.

God not only works in your life through prayer; He also works through *the Bible:*

> I Thessalonians 2:13: For this cause also thank we God without ceasing, because, when ye received the word of God which ye heard of us, ye received it not as the word of men, but as it is in truth, the word of God, which effectually worketh also in you that believe.

There it is—*God works in you through the Word of God.* "For the Word of God is quick, [living] and powerful," says Hebrews 4:12; and that life and power can be yours! Pay attention to the verbs in that verse. Paul doesn't say that Christians merely listened to the Word, or read it; he says that they *received* it and *believed* it. To receive the Word means that you say, "That's for me!" Then you go out and obey what it says. When your pastor or Sunday school teacher is explaining the Bible, you can either let it "go in one ear and out the other," or you can give it your full attention, take it into your mind and heart, and trust the Spirit to use it to work in your life. Really, this is a miracle, and it's difficult to explain it! But you can certainly *experience* it if you will open your heart and mind to the Bible, believe it, and obey it.

It isn't just the *hearing* and *reading* of the Bible that the Spirit uses; He also works when you *memorize* Scripture and hide it in your heart. In Luke 8:11 Jesus compared your Bible to seed—and seed bears no fruit until it is planted and watered. When you memorize a new verse and understand what it means, and when you obey it in your life, the Spirit uses that verse to strengthen you and make you more like Christ.

The third "tool" the Spirit uses to work in your life is *suffering*. I Peter 4:12-14 puts it this way:

> Beloved, think it not strange concerning the fiery trial which is to try you, as though some strange thing happened unto you: But rejoice, inasmuch as ye are partakers of Christ's sufferings; . . . for the spirit of glory and of God resteth upon you. . . .

The Holy Spirit works in your life when you allow God to put you through uncomfortable circumstances *for Christ's sake*. This doesn't mean that the Spirit works when you suffer because of sin or because you are out of the will of God! It does mean that God uses the "furnace of suffering" to melt and purify you so that He can mold you into a Christian who will glorify Him. This "furnace" may be ridicule or scoffing from the crowd at school; or it may be misunderstanding on the part of unsaved friends. Whatever it is, if you are "reproached for the name of Christ" you can be sure that the Spirit will be there to work in your life and give you joy in the midst of suffering.

You can see, then, how the Spirit works in you. First, He reveals a truth to you from the Word. You pray about this truth until it becomes a part of your "inner man." Then God puts you through some circumstance to test you; and if you trust in that truth from the Word, you will come through with flying colors. But if you give up when the furnace is turned on, the Spirit will stop working; and you'll go backward in your spiritual life.

Remember how this principle operated in Joseph's life? Joseph knew from God's Word that he would one day rule over his brethren; yet there he lay in an Egyptian prison. How Satan tried his faith! But Joseph was a man of prayer and the Spirit used the Word to build him up. And one day he was whisked out of the dungeon and placed on the throne!

This same principle also operated in David's life. As a teen-ager David had been anointed king; but Saul was still on the throne. Then Saul tried to kill David! God used those difficult circumstances to work in David's life and to prepare him for the great work that lay ahead.

God wants to work *through* you, but He can't work *through* you until He first works *in* you. He is more concerned about what you *are* than about what you *do,* because if your Christian character is right, your service will be right. If you spend time daily with your Bible, if you have a consistent prayer life, and if you allow God to bring whatever circumstances He wishes into your life, then He will be able to work *in* and *through* you for His glory.

And your life will be a miracle!

10

Timothy—
Service With a Smile!

WHEN I GET to heaven, I want to thank
the Apostle Paul for at least two things. First,
I want to thank him for being obedient to
God and taking the gospel to Europe. If he
hadn't obeyed, I might not have been saved!

Then, I want to thank him for the way he
helped Timothy. Not every older Christian is
interested in young people and Timothy was
probably in his teens when Paul enlisted him
as a part of his missionary team. Paul didn't
have this "younger generation" attitude; he
believed in young Timothy and gave him
every chance to grow and prove himself in the
Lord's work. I wonder where our churches
would be today if every adult Christian
"adopted" a Timothy of his own?

As you know from reading your New Testament, Paul wrote two letters to Timothy. Paul had been arrested in Jerusalem and taken to Rome for trial. He had been released after a couple of years, and he and his associates had visited again the churches they had founded, among them the church at Ephesus (Paul had pastored there for three years). The situation at Ephesus was discouraging: false teachers had come in and the good work Paul had done was rapidly being weakened. Paul left young Timothy there to fight the battle while he went on to other churches; and it was from one of those churches he wrote I Timothy to encourage Timothy and help him in his pastoral work. Paul was then arrested again and taken to Rome; it was from his Roman prison that he wrote II Timothy, the last letter he ever wrote.

As you read these two very personal letters they seem like Paul's own photograph albums, picturing his many associations with Timothy. Without much effort, you can find in these two letters at least five pictures of Timothy that illustrate what every Christian teen-ager ought to be.

Timothy the Son. ". . . my own son in the faith," is the way Paul addressed him (I Timothy 1:2), because Paul had helped to win Timothy to Jesus Christ.

Timothy's mother was a Jewess but his father was a Gentile. We read nothing about his father's religion, but Paul does tell us that Timothy's mother and grandmother were believers: "When I call to remembrance the unfeigned [sincere] faith that is in thee, which dwelt first in thy grandmother Lois, and thy mother Eunice . . ." (II Timothy 1:5).

Timothy, his mother, and his grandmother (and possibly his father, but we aren't sure) lived in the area around Derbe and Lystra, probably in the city of Lystra itself. Paul visited there on his first missionary journey (Acts 14:1ff) and was stoned by the people because he refused to let them worship him. It was at that time Lois and Eunice were saved, and then young Timothy (probably a lad of seven or eight).

Immediately Paul was drawn to the boy; he claimed him as his "son in the faith." Little did Timothy realize that his decision to follow Christ would open up for him an exciting, rewarding life that would write his name on the pages of the Bible and the pages of history! I'm sure some of his Jewish and Greek friends ridiculed his faith in Christ; but Timothy stayed true to his Lord and his friend, Paul.

Timothy the Servant. But what happened to Timothy after Paul left town? For one thing, he started learning the Word of God. "And that from a child thou hast known the holy scriptures," Paul reminded him in II Timothy 3:15. And Timothy identified himself with the local church and began to grow. When Paul came back to town five or six years later, he discovered that young Timothy, now a teen-ager, was "well reported of by the brethren that were at Lystra and Iconium" (Acts 16:2).

This is important: *Timothy had stayed home and proved himself among his own family and friends.* He wasn't like some young people I've met who want to "turn the world upside down" three weeks after they're saved! It's wonderful to have that kind of zeal, but unless zeal is balanced with spiritual knowledge and experience, it can do more harm than good. When Paul was advising Timothy on his pastoral duties at Ephesus, he wrote concerning church officers: "Not a novice [beginner], lest being lifted up with pride he fall into the condemnation of the devil. . . . And let these also first be proved . . ." (I Timothy 3:6 and 10). You may wonder why your pastor or church officers don't brag about you and your Christian friends, or give you places of prestige or glory in the church. The reason is simple: they know you aren't ready for it. First you have to prove yourself, and then God will open the doors for public service.

It doesn't take any imagination to picture

our teen-aged Timothy as a Christian in Lystra. He was growing spiritually and physically. I'm sure he faced the same temptations you face today, and those I faced as a teen-ager. *But he was learning how to serve;* he was developing a servant's mind, a concern for other people and their needs. Paul wrote of Timothy: "For I have no man likeminded, who will naturally care for your state" (Philippians 2:20). Unlike his teen-age friends, Timothy was thinking of others, not himself; and because of that, God opened a marvelous door for him.

Timothy the Substitute. When Paul and Silas came to Lystra on their second journey, they needed another helper. John Mark had deserted them on their first trip (Acts 13:13) and Paul had been unwilling to take him on this second journey (Acts 15:36-41). We'll find out in heaven whether Paul was right or wrong! But he and Silas needed another helper, someone who was humble enough to do the menial jobs that would release them to preach the gospel.

They found their man at Lystra: young Timothy. He was Mark's substitute.

Paul makes it very clear that John Mark finally got straightened out and became "profitable . . . for the ministry" (II Timothy 4:11). In fact, he wrote our Gospel of Mark! But just think of what Mark missed when he turned his back on God's call and returned to Jerusalem! Though he had his times of fears and tears, Timothy "stayed by the stuff" and remained faithful to God.

John Mark and Timothy illustrate an important truth that you'll want to learn: *Don't rush into Christian service until you're prepared for it.* I'm afraid John Mark left home unprepared. Barnabas, Paul's companion, was his uncle (Colossians 4:10), and Mark and Barnabas had accompanied Paul in his mission of mercy to Jerusalem when he took relief to the famine-stricken saints (Acts 11:27-30; 12:25). But John Mark had not really proved himself at home, and when the going got rough, he took the easy way out. As a young man he was probably proud of his associations with the great Apostle Paul—and pride is the very thing a new believer has to watch out for. "Not a novice [beginner], lest being lifted up with pride he fall . . . ," warns I Timothy 3:6.

Timothy began as a substitute, but he remained a co-laborer with Paul for nearly twenty years. You and I would know nothing about Timothy had he stayed in Lystra and refused to obey God's call. Because he gave his all to Christ, God honored him. ". . . He that doeth the will of God abideth for ever," promises I John 2:17.

Are you going to fill that place of service

God has for you? Or is somebody going to be your substitute?

Timothy the Soldier. Paul was fond of using military and athletic terms. He often mentions running, wrestling, boxing, and other athletic activities; and he also uses military terms to teach spiritual truths. That's why he wrote to young Timothy: "Thou therefore endure hardness, as a good soldier of Jesus Christ" (II Timothy 2:3). Paul didn't suggest that Timothy enlist in the army of Christ; he informed him that *he already was a soldier!* The Christian life isn't a playground; it's a battleground.

Expect battles. Don't go out and deliberately start them, but expect them. "Yea, and all that will live godly in Christ Jesus shall suffer persecution" (II Timothy 3:12). Because you belong to Christ and live for Him, the world hates you and so does Satan. You can be sure that God will give you the strength you need to face the enemies and fight the battles, so "be strong in the grace that is in Christ Jesus" (II Timothy 2:1)!

One thing above all that is demanded of soldiers is *loyalty.* "No man that warreth entangleth himself with the affairs of this life; that he may please him who hath chosen him to be a soldier," says II Timothy 2:4. Perhaps you have heard about the Confederate soldier who did watch-repairing on the side.

His unit had been stationed away from the battle for several weeks and business was booming. Then one day the order came through the camp: "Pack up! We move in one hour!" The watchmaker rushed up to his commander and cried, "But I can't go into battle! I have too many watches to finish!" His commander calmly replied, "You were called to be a soldier, not a watchmaker!" One man's entanglements almost cost an army the battle.

A loyal Christian soldier isn't going to get entangled with the world—this would make him a traitor, because the world is Christ's enemy! Paul knew a soldier like that and mentioned him in II Timothy 4:10: "For Demas hath forsaken me, having loved this present world. . . ." Young Samson allowed himself (*and* his hair) to get entangled with the enemy, and he ended up a blind prisoner in the enemy dungeon. Read Judges 16 if you've forgotten.

How does a Christian soldier become entangled with the world? There are three dangerous steps:

". . . the *friendship* of the world . . ." (James 4:4)
"*Love* not the world . . ." (I John 2:15)

". . . be not *conformed* to this world . . ." (Romans 12:2)

Friends, lovers, imitators—and before the soldier knows it he has betrayed his own Captain of Salvation!

"I have fought a good fight . . . ," Paul wrote Timothy at the end of his life (II Timothy 4:7). What better record could a Christian soldier have?

Timothy the Steward. A steward is a person who guards and invests his master's wealth. His main responsibility is to be faithful and be able to give a good account to his master.

Paul was a steward of the message of the gospel. "According to the glorious gospel of the blessed God, which was committed to my trust," he wrote in I Timothy 1:11. What did Paul do with this priceless treasure? He, in turn, gave it to Timothy! His last words in I Timothy 6:20 are, "O Timothy, keep that which is committed to thy trust. . . ."

What was Timothy to do with that sacred trust? He was to pass it on to others! "And the things that thou hast heard of me among many witnesses, the same commit thou to faithful men, who shall be able to teach others also" (II Timothy 2:2). God gave the treasure to Paul; Paul entrusted it to Timothy; and Timothy was to entrust it to faithful men who, in turn, would commit it to others. That is how the Word of God came to us!

Suppose Timothy had been an unfaithful steward? Suppose he had not heeded Paul's warning in II Timothy 1:13-14: "Hold fast the form of sound words, which thou hast heard of me. . . . That good thing which was committed unto thee keep by the Holy Ghost which dwelleth in us"? What might have happened? Well, for one thing, there would have been multitudes of people who never would have heard the Word of God. The church Timothy served would have become weaker and weaker and finally passed off the scene. What a tragedy!

Put yourself in Timothy's place, not as the pastor of a church, but as a young person who has been given the treasure of the Christian faith. *What are you doing with it?* Are you guarding your faith, valuing it above everything else? Or is it just as "second-hand" faith to you? How much is your Bible worth to you? How much do you value your church, your pastor, his sermons, your Christian heritage? *You are a Christian steward, and God is depending on you to guard His spiritual treasure and pass it on to others!*

It goes without saying that Satan would like to rob you of your treasure, and he uses four devices to do it. First, he tries *false doc-*

trine. "But evil men and seducers shall wax worse and worse, deceiving, and being deceived," Paul warns in II Timothy 3:13. If he can get you to read a pamphlet by some member of a false cult, or a book by some professor who denies the Word of God; or if he can introduce you to a follower of a false doctrine, then he is on the way toward stealing your treasure from you. Watch out for false doctrine, no matter who presents it. In the very next verse, Paul says, "But continue thou in the things which thou hast learned and hast been assured of. . . ." Listen to your parents, your pastor, your teachers as they ground you in the Word of God, and you will be a faithful steward, guarding the treasure from Satan's grasp.

The devil's second device is *false values.* "For the love of money is the root of all [kinds of] evil: which while some coveted after, they have erred [been seduced] from the faith . . . ," warns I Timothy 6:10. The Christian who starts living by the sign of the dollar instead of the sign of the cross is heading for trouble. Many a Christian teen-ager has gone off to college determined to be a faithful steward and train for service, only to have a "big offer" come his way at graduation time and make him give up his calling for an attractive salary, home, and position. If anything in this world becomes more important to you than the spiritual values of Christ and the Bible, you are in danger of losing the treasure.

Satan's third device is *false knowledge*. "O Timothy, keep that which is committed to thy trust, avoiding profane and vain babblings, and oppositions of science [knowledge] falsely so called: Which some professing have erred concerning the faith" warns I Timothy 6:20-21. Paul isn't criticizing true science, but false knowledge—the empty philosophies of the day. How easy it is for young minds to get excited over man's wisdom and philosophy! Any knowledge that contradicts the Bible and causes you to stray from the faith is *false* knowledge, and it is poison! ". . . let God be true, but every man a liar," writes Paul in Romans 3:4; and Psalm 119:128 reads, "Therefore I esteem all thy precepts concerning all things to be right; and I hate every false way."

The devil's final device is *false living*. If he can get the Christian steward to profess one thing but practice another, he has won the battle. "Holding faith, and a good conscience," Paul writes in I Timothy 1:19, "which some having put away [conscience] concerning faith have made shipwreck." The fastest way to wreck your spiritual life is to violate your conscience, that inner judge God has given you to let you know when you have done something wrong. Your conscience is a tender thing and can be easily changed from a *good* conscience into a *defiled* conscience (Titus 1:15), then a *seared* (calloused) conscience (I Timothy 4:2) that no longer functions. And all of this happens to the Christian who does not live what he professes to believe. He carries secret sins in his heart and practices them when he thinks he can get away with it. He is an unfaithful steward, and before long Satan takes the treasure away from him. He is left empty-handed, with nothing to pass on to others.

"I have kept the faith," Paul testified in his last letter from that Roman prison (II Timothy 4:7). He was a faithful steward—as was young Timothy, his son in the faith.

"Moreover it is required in stewards, that a man be found faithful" (I Corinthians 4:2). I hope that includes you and me!

11

Christ—
the Perfect Teen-ager

A FEW CHAPTERS ago we discovered that the Prodigal Son was a failure and certainly not the best example for a teen-ager to follow—except in repentance and a willingness to come home and be forgiven. But have you ever thought of comparing Jesus Christ and the Prodigal Son?

For example, both of them left home. The Prodigal left for selfish reasons, of course, while Christ left heaven because He loves us. And both of them became poor; the Prodigal because he lived in sin, and Christ because He wanted to make us rich. (Read II Corinthians 8:9 in your Bible.) Both of them died. Of course, the Prodigal "died" in a figurative sense (Luke 15:24), while Christ died literally for our sins. Both were joyfully welcomed home by their fathers.

But that's about the extent of it. You'll have an easier time *contrasting* these two sons than you will comparing them! One was a sinner, the other a Saviour. One was selfishly independent; the other said, "I do always those things that please Him (the Father)." The Prodigal spent all he had on sin; Christ gave all He had to save us from sin. The Prodigal led others into sin; Jesus leads people out of sin and into salvation. The Prodigal started out a son and ended up a servant, while Christ came as a Servant in order to make us sons of God.

What was wrong with that Jewish boy in Christ's parable? Well, for one thing, there was something mentally wrong with him. I don't mean that he had a low IQ or was unbalanced. It was just that he couldn't think straight. His mind was so filled with his own importance and his own plans that nobody could change him. To use a common phrase, he was "beside himself." That's why Luke 15:17 says, "And when he came to himself. . . ." The turning point in his life was in his mind: *he came to himself.*

There was also something physically wrong with the boy. No, he wasn't a cripple; there is no evidence that there was even a blemish on his body. Chances are he was a handsome, popular Jewish boy with a knack for making friends. The trouble was that *he lived for his body*. Christ says that he "wasted his substance with riotous living" (Luke 15:13). Instead of controlling his body, his body controlled him. ". . . whose god is their belly, . . . who mind earthly things," is the way Paul describes this kind of person in Philippians 3:19.

The Prodigal had another problem: there was something socially wrong with him. He couldn't get along with his father or his older brother. He didn't know how to make friends on the basis of his own personality; he had to throw parties and bribe people with his money. When the money ran out, the friends disappeared—and left him with the pigs!

But at the bottom of all his problems was the *spiritual* need: he was spiritually "dead" and "lost." Don't forget that a teen-ager (or an adult, for that matter) can be physically alive but spiritually dead, without God's life within. And the Prodigal Son was "lost" (separated from God) long before he arrived in "The Far Country." "Lost" and "dead"— what a tragic condition to be in!

There are thousands of teens today who idolize people just like the Prodigal Son! Compare this boy with the popular teen matinee idols who have little or no time for God, who glorify sex and exciting escapades, who win a following because of what they have, not what they are. And the people who follow them *become just like them!* That's why it's important that you fix your eyes on the best possible examples; and the Perfect Example for you to follow as a teen-ager is your Saviour, Jesus Christ.

The other day I heard a TV commercial about a doll called "The Ideal Teen." She has clothes, a car, boyfriends and girlfriends, lots of exciting things (her own TV set, a typewriter, a radio, a boat, etc.), and she's the most popular teen on campus. Well, maybe she *is* an "ideal teen"; but she certainly isn't *my* ideal of a teen-ager! If owning three closets full of clothes, a TV set, a camera, and a typewriter, and if hypnotizing every boy in town is an honest description of an ideal teen, there are very few "ideal teens" in this world! The tragedy is that the youngsters who play with this doll may grow up thinking that the ideal teen life is made up of excitement and things.

No, if you're looking for an ideal teen-ager, look at Jesus Christ. Here is the record of His life at the age of twelve, just before He entered His teen years:

> *Luke 2:39-52:* And when they had performed all things according to the law of the Lord, they returned into Galilee,

to their own city Nazareth. 40 And the child grew, and waxed strong in spirit, filled with wisdom: and the grace of God was upon him. 41 Now his parents went to Jerusalem every year at the feast of the passover. 42 And when he was twelve years old, they went up to Jerusalem after the custom of the feast. 43 And when they had fulfilled the days, as they returned, the child Jesus tarried behind in Jerusalem; and Joseph and his mother knew not of it. 44 But they, supposing him to have been in the company, went a day's journey; and they sought him among their kinsfolk and acquaintance. 45 And when they found him not, they turned back again to Jerusalem, seeking him. 46 And it came to pass, that after three days they found him in the temple, sitting in the midst of the doctors, both hearing them, and asking them questions. 47 And all that heard him were astonished at his understanding and answers. 48 And when they saw him, they were amazed: and his mother said unto him, Son, why hast thou thus dealt with us? behold, thy father and I have sought thee sorrowing. 49 And he said unto them, How is it that ye sought me? wist ye not that I must be about my Father's business? 50 And they understood not the saying which he spake unto them. 51 And he went down with them, and came to Nazareth, and was subject unto them: but his mother kept all these sayings in her heart. 52 And Jesus increased in wisdom and stature, and in favour with God and man.

There were several problems that Jesus faced in His teen years that perhaps you might even face; yet He won the battles just the same. For one thing, He lived in a difficult city, Nazareth, in the despised area known as Galilee. The Jews in Judea despised "Galilee of the Gentiles" and Nazareth in particular.

His earthly father, Joseph, was a poor man, a carpenter, so Jesus had no luxuries when He was a Child and a Teen-ager. Luke 2:24 informs us that Joseph was too poor to bring a lamb or a goat for a sacrifice; instead, he brought the most inexpensive sacrifice—turtledoves and pigeons.

Christ's brothers and sisters didn't believe in Him (John 7:1-5 and Mark 6:1-5); and his own mother Mary didn't always understand Him (Mark 3:31-35), nor did Joseph (Luke 2:50). If you've even complained, "Nobody in this house understands me!" just keep in mind that Jesus was misunderstood *all His earthly life!*

In spite of those handicaps, Jesus Christ stands out as the Ideal Teen-ager—the Perfect Teen-ager. "And Jesus increased in wisdom and stature, and in favour with God and man," says Luke 2:52. In other words, Christ was a *balance*d Teen-ager: mentally (*wisdom*), physically (*stature*), spiritually (*favor with God*), and socially (*and with man*). Everything that the Prodigal Son was *not*, Jesus is! The Prodigal was "out of balance" mentally, physically, socially, and spiritually; and that's why he's a poor example to follow. But when you pattern yourself after Jesus Christ, you are following the only Perfect Pattern God has ever given men.

Jesus grew in the four important areas of life.

Mentally: When a Jewish boy became six years of age, his mother took him to the local synagogue where he was taught the Jewish Law and the traditions of the Jewish rabbis. This was his elementary education. When he became ten years of age, the rabbi started to prepare him for his *Bar Mitzvah* at the age of thirteen, when he became a "son of the law" (which is what *Bar Mitzvah* means) and had an adult standing in the home and community.

Nowhere does the Bible put a premium on ignorance. In fact, one of the constant commandments in the Book of Proverbs is: "Get wisdom! Hold fast to knowledge!" This includes not only an understanding of the Bible, but also an understanding of the world God made and the things that are in it. If you aren't doing your best at school, then your life will get out of balance. Perhaps God didn't give you the mental equipment to be class valedictorian; but certainly He gave you sufficient tools to pass and keep up a respectable average! If you plan to major in football, keep in mind that even a quarterback has to know how to count!

The fact of the matter is, the Christian student who fails to do his best work is a poor testimony for Christ.

Physically: The word "stature" in Luke 2:52 really means "age," but it carries with it the idea of growth and development. Our Lord took care of His body and allowed nothing to harm it. And as His earthly father's Helper in the carpenter shop (Mark 6:3—"Is not this the carpenter . . . ?") Jesus learned how to carry burdens and develop skills. The rabbis taught that every father owed it to his son to teach him a trade. "He that knows not a trade will become a thief!"

It goes without saying that the Christian teen-ager needs to develop and care for his body. After all, your body is *God's temple,* according to I Corinthians 6:19-20; *God's tool,* according to Romans 6:13; and *God's testing ground,* according to I Corinthians 9:24-27. God dwells in your body; God uses your body in His service; and God tests your dedication and devotion by the way you use your body.

It's tragic the way some of today's teens abuse their bodies as they pattern their lives after the "popularity people" of their teen world. Late hours, poor diets, bad habits, impure appetites—all of these tear down the body and throw the life out of balance.

Socially: "And he went down with them, and came to Nazareth, and was subject unto them . . ." is the way Luke 2:51 describes Christ's relationship to His parents. (Of course, Joseph was His *legal* father, not His real father in the physical sense.) The first test of your social abilities is right at home! As a Teen-ager, Jesus knew what it was to respect and honor His parents, and to obey them. "Children, obey your parents in the Lord: for this is right" (Ephesians 6:1). "Children, obey your parents in all things: for this is well pleasing unto the Lord" (Colossians 3:20).

(No wonder that at the end of thirty years, when Jesus stepped into His public ministry, His Father could say from heaven: "This is my beloved Son, in whom I am well pleased" —Matthew 3:17.)

But Jesus not only got along with His family at home; He also knew how to behave at the Temple. Luke tells of Christ's visit to the Temple at the age of twelve, when He amazed the rabbis with His knowledge of the Word. And from the way the common people gravitated toward Jesus during His earthly ministry, it isn't hard to believe that, as a Boy, He had many friends and neighborhood companions. Please don't get the idea that the teen-aged Jesus walked about Nazareth in a pious way, with a halo glowing over His head! Certainly He lived a spotless life, since He was the very Son of God; but He lived a *balanced* life, and that included social fellowship with His family and friends.

Spiritually: This, of course, is the key to a balanced life. If God is where He ought to be, then everything else will fall into place. ". . . seek ye first the kingdom of God, and his righteousness; and all these things shall be added unto you," promises Matthew 6:33. Naturally, Jesus did not have to be saved, since He was the perfect Son of God. But as a Man, He did have to depend on His Father for guidance and strength day by day.

What a perfect Example He is for your spiritual life! He was always in the synagogue on the sabbath, even though He opposed its false teachings and practices. He depended a great deal on prayer. In fact, Luke tells us of seven specific times when Jesus prayed; and sometimes He spent all night in prayer. Think of His knowledge of the Bible! Whether Satan was tempting Him or the enemy opposing Him, He always had just the right verse to settle the matter.

If you want to live a balanced life as a Christian teen-ager, then you must use Christ as your Example. As you read the Bible—and the Gospels in particular—you see Him in every circumstance of life; and you discover that following "in His steps" always leads to happiness and victory.

Don't stop with "following Christ" as your Example, as wonderful as this is! Go one step further and let the Holy Spirit *make you like Christ!* You'll remember in our visit with Mary that we discovered that the Holy Spirit dwells within you—"Christ liveth in me!" And if you follow His directions, the Spirit will transform you *from within* to be more and more like Jesus Christ.

It starts with *dedication*—the Romans 12:1-2 kind of dedication that we discovered when we met Daniel. As you *daily* surrender your body, mind, and will to Christ, the Spirit transforms you into Christ's image. In your attitudes, actions, and appetites, you will be Christ-like.

II Corinthians 3:18 gives you another secret:

But we all, with open [unveiled] face beholding as in a glass [mirror] the glory of the Lord, are changed into the same image from glory to glory, even as by the Spirit of the Lord.

A complicated verse, isn't it? It means that when the child of God spends time daily with the Word of God (here compared to a mirror), the Spirit of God reveals Christ to him and *transforms him to be like Christ!* When you look into a glass mirror, you see yourself—blemishes and all. But when you look into the Bible—God's mirror—you see Christ, and as you receive His Word into your heart, the Spirit performs that miracle of transformation, making you more and more like Him.

A spiritual Christian is always a *balanced* Christian. When you become more like Christ, you will be better physically, socially, and mentally, as well as spiritually. Of course, this doesn't mean that Christ will give you the strongest body on campus, the keenest mind, or the most friends. It does mean that He will take what you have—mentally, physically, socially, and spiritually—and develop it in a balanced way to its highest degree.

Which "son" are you following as *your* example: the Prodigal Son—or the Perfect Son, Jesus Christ?

12

Don't Just
Grow Old—Grow Up!

"WHY DON'T YOU act your age?"

How many times have you heard that question?

Frankly, it's difficult for a teen-ager to "act his age" because being a teen-ager usually means jumping from one extreme to another. One day you wish you were back in grade school, protected from the problems of life. The next day you can't understand why Dad won't buy you a car of your own!

Part of the confusion and frustration of your teen years (and some teens have more than others) rests right here. In every way— physically, mentally, socially, and spiritually —you're moving from the dependence of childhood into the responsibilities and privileges of adulthood, and sometimes the bridge seems to shake. The important thing is this: don't just grow old—*grow up!* You can't help growing older; nature takes care of that. But too many people who have grown old have never grown up; they're just as childish and immature today as they were in the fifth grade.

Maturity is a word you hear a lot as a teenager. It's one of those words that isn't easy to define in a practical way. A mature person is one who has accepted himself, and who understands himself and his world, and who uses his life creatively for his own good, the good of others, and the glory of God. That's a long definition, so we'd better take it a step at a time.

A mature person *accepts himself*. He has taken a long, honest look into the mirror, and he doesn't argue with what he sees. Of course, he tries to better himself in every way possible, but he doesn't argue with his looks, his talents, or his handicaps. He doesn't live in a dream world where he's always the hero and where there are never any problems.

He also *understands himself*. A famous Greek once said, "The unexamined life is not worth living." To be sure, nobody *really* knows his own heart; but at the same time, nobody can afford *not* to try to understand what makes him "tick." If you avoid facing the brutal facts of your own personality, you will never mature. But if you try to understand your fears and frustrations, your desires and disappointments, you will be that much further along the road to maturity.

The mature person also understands *his world,* problems and all. He doesn't necessarily understand *everything* in his world, but he certainly has a good grasp of the situation. The maturing teen-ager tries to understand his home and what it means to his life; his school and the crowd he runs with; and his church and the things it stands for. This understanding of his teen world gives him a sense of stability: he knows who he is and where he is and why things happen the way they do. He learns to accept the occasional family disagreements because he realizes that his growing up is as much a challenge to his parents as it is to him!

Finally, the mature person is a builder; he uses his life *creatively* for his own good, the good of others, and the glory of God. He doesn't deliberately tear himself or others down, nor does he deliberately disgrace Christ. He realizes that his life is bound up with the lives of others, that "no man is an island." He directs his life and uses his talents to better himself and others, and to honor his God.

This, then, is maturity—this process of growing up while you grow older. It isn't an easy process; there are always growing pains. And it isn't a simple process, because one area of your life might mature faster than another. But it's an exciting process, a life-long adventure! And if you are going to be a *real* teen-ager, not an artificial adult, you'll accept the privileges and responsibilities of maturity with confidence and courage.

The lives of the six Bible teens we've met in this book point the way to real success in the matter of maturity. They illustrate for you the six essentials for maturity in your teen years.

First, we met Joseph; and we learned that there can be no success without *discipline*. The undisciplined teen-ager will never be a mature adult. Discipline means service, self-control, and suffering. The teen-ager who resents work (whether at home or school), who refuses to discipline his body and mind, and who steers clear of difficult circumstances, will never grow up. He'll be a pampered adult who expects everybody to live to please him—and he'll be miserable!

David taught us another lesson: there can be no success without *diligence*. There must be purpose in life or life isn't worth living. David was faithful with a few things, so God gave him many things. He was diligent as a servant, so God made him a ruler. He was faithful when it came to hard work, so God rewarded him with joy. Maturity doesn't come automatically; it's the result of diligence on your part in every area of your life. Laziness or carelessness during your teen years will show up in your adult years in one way or another.

Maturity depends not only on discipline and diligence; it also depends on *decision,* the kind of decision that Daniel displayed. You can go along with the crowd and take the so-called easy way if you want to; or you can decide to be a transformer, not a conformer. Your life is made up of decisions and the consequences of those decisions, so that, for the most part, you are weaving your own pattern. "But I find it hard to make the right decisions!" I hear you say. Of course you do; *every* Christian fights this battle.

But that's where our next Bible teen comes in; for Mary explains the secret of spiritual *dynamic.* ". . . it is God which worketh in you both to will and to do of his good pleasure" (Philippians 2:13). The Holy Spirit can work in your life and lift you from the ordinary to the extraordinary and make you into a miracle! When you allow the Spirit to use the Bible, prayer, and circumstances (*suffering,* in particular), then God will work *in* you and *through* you.

Timothy illustrates the fifth essential for maturity: *determination.* How many times he wanted to quit! And how many times Paul prayed for him and tried to encourage him! "Be a courageous soldier!" Paul wrote. "Guard the treasure I've given you!" Paul was going to be martyred, and he knew that Timothy would have to step in and take his place. Have you ever considered the fact that some day in the future *you* may be called on to take another Christian's place? Your godly determination today in your teen years will prepare you for that opportunity tomorrow.

Of course, maturity implies development to the full, and there must be a pattern or *design* to guide you; and this Perfect Design is Jesus Christ. "That we . . . may grow up unto him in all things . . ." (Ephesians 4:14-15).

There are dozens of "teen-age idols" you can use as the pattern for your life, but none of them can begin to compare with Jesus Christ. The Holy Spirit within you wants to work in you to make you like Christ. Instead of being conformed to the world (Romans 12:2), you want to be "conformed to the image of his Son" (Romans 8:29). What greater Example could you follow?

These, then, are the six essentials for maturity: discipline, diligence, decision, dynamic, determination, and design. And you've seen from the lives of six Bible teen-agers that these essentials *really work!* And when they work, they make you a *real* teen-ager!

In other words, there may be many things in your life that seem to be handicaps. Perhaps you have physical handicaps; perhaps there are problems at home or at school. The Bible teens had their problems and handicaps, too; but *God used those handicaps to make them successes instead of failures!* Because the Bible young people followed the basic principles that make for success and maturity, they had happy, useful lives and were able to help others (including us today!) for their good and for God's glory.

Don't just grow old—*grow up!* Be a real teen-ager today, and you'll become a real adult tomorrow—a Christian adult ready for the challenges and enjoyments God has prepared for you.